iPhone Guide

The Complete Beginners and Seniors Manual to Master the New iPhone SE (2020) and Tips and Tricks for iOS 13

Aaron Madison

Copyright © 2020 by Aaron Madison - All rights reserved.

This book is copyright, and no part may be reproduced or transmitted through any means, be it mechanical, electronic, internet, or otherwise without the permission of the publisher except in brief quotation or review of the book.

Table of Contents

INTRODUCTION 1
CHAPTER ONE 2
Features of iPhone SE 2020 2
Set Up iPhone SE (2020) 7
How to Set up Touch ID 11
Restore from iCloud Backup 12
Turn On iCloud Backup 13
How to Reset iPhone 14
How to Turn ON/OFF iPhone 15
How to Enable Emergency SOS 16
How to Create a New Apple ID 17
    Change Apple ID on the iPhone 20
Set Up Apple Pay 21
    Configure Apple Pay on the iPhone 21
CHAPTER TWO 23
Show Previews on the Lock Screen 23
How to Use a Wireless or USB Mouse 24
    Tips for Using the Mouse 26
    Customize the Buttons on the Mouse 27
Customize AssistiveTouch 27
CHAPTER THREE 29
Customize Text Message Tones 29
Set Your Notification Preferences 30

Set Messages to Share Your Personalized Contact Data 30

Turn on Text, Call, and FaceTime forwarding ... 31

Filter Unknown Calls and Messages 31

Set Location Preferences Apps 32

How to Enable iCloud Keychain on iPhone 34

    How to Access iCloud Keychain Passwords .. 35

How to Activate Siri 36

    Activate Siri with Side Button 36

    How to Exit Siri 36

    Change Siri's language 36

CHAPTER FOUR 37

Change iPhone's Language 37

How to Scan Documents in the Files App 39

How to Use iMessage Search 39

Share Photos Without Location Information ... 40

Remove App Size Limitations on Cellular Data 40

How to Take Long Screenshots of Websites 41

Customize Notification Centre 42

How to Switch Apps 45

Display Multitasking Quick App Switcher 45

Force Quit Apps 46

How to Access Reachability Mode 46

How to Access Control Center 47

CHAPTER FIVE 48

Set Up Monthly Cycle Data 48

Customize Cycle Tracking Options 50
Receive Period Predictions and Notifications .. 52
Set Up Fertility Predictions and Notifications . 54
Manage Menstruation Flow 55
Add Cycle Symptoms to Cycle Tracking 56
Remove Cycle Tracking Data 56
Disable True Tone Display 57
How to Enable/Disable Tap to Wake 57
Set Up Haptic Touch 58
How to Use Sign In with Apple Feature 59
Share Your Location Using the Apple Map 60
CHAPTER SIX 61
How to Use Memoji Feature 61
   How to Create Memoji 63
   Edit, Delete or Create Another Memoji 64
   How to Remove Memoji Option 66
How to Use Siri Shortcuts 68
   Add Shortcuts to Siri 68
   Add Shortcut from a third-party App 69
   Add Shortcut from Settings 69
   Delete a shortcut or change the phrase 70
How to Set Screen Time 71
   Restrict Functions of Apps 71
   Restrict Use of Contents 71
   Restrict Access to Websites 72

Change Screen Brightness 73
   Turn on Automatic Brightness Adjustment .. 73
Shorten Automatic Lock 73
CHAPTER SEVEN 74
How to Change Wallpaper 74
Add Widget to Display the Battery Level as a Percentage 74
How to Control Offload Unused Apps 75
Restrict Offload Unused Apps 76
Move Home Screen Apps 76
   Moving Apps to Another Page 77
Create a Folder on the Home Screen 78
Reset Icon Layout on Home Screen 78
Enable Location Services on Find My App 79
   Locate Family/Friends on Find My App 80
   Share Your Location via Find My App 81
   Enable Offline Finding via Find My App 81
   Verify Offline Finding is Turned On 82
How to Create a New Reminder 83
   Receive Notification When Sending Message via Reminder App 84
   Remove Reminder 84
   Creating Grouped Lists via Reminder App ... 85
   Add New Subtasks to Reminder 86
   Tag a Contact in the Reminder App 87
CHAPTER EIGHT 88

Enable/Disable Swipe Typing............................ 88
How to Use Swipe Type 88
Set a Custom Name and Profile Picture via iMessage... 89
    Share Custom Name and Profile Photo 91
    Delete your iMessage Profile Image............... 93
Pair a DualShock 4 Controller with Your iPhone 94
Pair Xbox One Controller With iPhone 94
Unpair DualShock 4/Xbox One S controller..... 95
How to Customize VoiceOver 96
CHAPTER NINE..97
Scan Documents from the Files App 97
Save and Share Webpage as a PDF................... 99
Enable Content Blockers in Safari 102
Temporarily Disable Content Blockers in Safari 102
Access the Download Manager in Safari 103
Change the Default Safari Download Location 104
How to Automatically Close All Open Safari Tabs 104
Enable/Disable Limit Ad Tracking.................. 105
Turn On Voice Control..................................... 106
How to Block Email Senders 107
How to Unblock a Number on iPhone............ 108
Unblock People Who Text You 108

How to Add Contacts on iPhone 109
Set Up Voicemail on your iPhone 109
How to Merge Duplicate iPhone Contacts 110
Copy Contacts from Social Networks & Email . 111
Set Up Emergency Medical ID 111
CONCLUSION 113
ABOUT AUTHOR 114

INTRODUCTION

The new iPhone SE (2020) - formerly iPhone 9 is the cheap iPhone that many were waiting for, and that will compete with the low-end Android phones.

The good stuff is that it has the same processor as the iPhone 11, the A13 Bionic.

The iPhone SE (2020) has a Retina display that does not use OLED technology, like the iPhone 11, instead uses IPS LCD, which is similar to the old iPhone XR or iPhone 8. Another interesting fact is that it has a haptic touch.

The memory options (RAM) for the new iPhone SE begin at just 64GB, but it is also available with 128GB and 256GB.

There are so many configurations, tips, and tricks to learn about the iPhone SE 2020. This guide will answer all your questions, help you set up the device, master all the configurations, and use your iPhone SE (2020) like a pro.

Also, this book includes images to help you quickly master your iPhone SE (2020) without stress. The interesting part is that this book is suitable for both beginners and experts of Apple iPhone devices.

CHAPTER ONE

Features of iPhone SE 2020

At first glance, the second-generation iPhone SE looks like the iPhone 8 from 2017. It comes in the same form factor, features the same screen, and has a Touch ID home button, even the same camera sensor.

Upon closer inspection, the new iPhone SE is not exactly the reborn iPhone 8. Oh no, it may look the same, but it comes with many of the latest iPhone 11 specs. And, most importantly, a price that is almost from the past, as this is not an expensive Apple phone.

So can a phone that is a mix of technology dating back to 2015 still be a hit in today's world? We believe that the new small iPhone will have great appeal for many. This is why.

Is iPhone SE the same as iPhone 8?

- Available in three colors variant: white, product red and black
- Size: 138 x 67 x 7.3 mm
- 4.7-inch Retina HD display
- Resolution: 1334 x 750
- Weight: 148 g
- Touch ID Start button
- 7MP FaceTime camera

- IP67 waterproof
- Lightning connector

This iPhone SE 2020 completely replaces the iPhone 8, so you'll hear some call it the iPhone 9.

This is not iPhone SE Plus in any way. It has a 4.7-inch screen (with True Tone and Haptic Touch), which means it's not as big as, for example, and the 6.5-inch screen on the iPhone 11 Pro Max.

The SE features a Touch ID-enabled home button located at the bottom of the screen, but without Face ID, which would require the company's TrueDepth technology. That means the 7-megapixel FaceTime front camera is fine for calls and selfies but does not support Face Login, Animoji, or Animated Memoji.

While Apple has moved to USB-C to charge its latest devices, the iPhone SE 2020 sticks to the Lightning port connector, just like the iPhone 8. That's how similar these devices are, even the iPhone 8 cases. They will adapt to the 2020 SE, although Apple and others will, of course, be happy to sell you an iPhone SE if you wish.

The second-generation SE also retains its waterproof status, meaning you can accidentally drop it into the hotel's bathroom or pool.

How is the iPhone SE's performance?

- 64GB, 128GB, 256GB storage options
- A13 Bionic processor

- Wi-Fi 6, 4G LTE
- No face identification
- Without U1 chip

So the new iPhone SE certainly looks like a 2017 device, but its internal technology is pretty 2020. There is the same A13 Bionic processor found in iPhone 11 and iPhone 11 Pro models. That's unexpected for a budget model but most welcome, as it means this phone slides fast when it performs a variety of tasks, from gaming, photo editing, to WhatsApp, and casual emails.

Connectivity comes in the form of Wi-Fi 6, 4G (via dual SIM with eSIM support), all pointing towards fast connectivity. Overall, the SE offers a flagship phone experience.

Though numerous Android phone manufacturers have delivered this type of product for years, Apple has never offered this in the past.

However, the SE doesn't have all of its iPhone 11 peers. In the SE smartphone, there are no multiple cameras, no Face IDs, no stereo speakers, no new U1 chip, and no Lidar sensor as it is with the iPad Pro, which, at this price, is what we would expect. It extends noticeably to SE, so if any of those features is a must, then you have the option to pay more for the device that best suits your needs.

What is the battery life of iPhone SE like?

- Same battery as iPhone 8
- Supports Qi open standard wireless charging
- Compatible 18W fast charge (charger sold separately)

Battery life always brings up that big question: "Will it help me get through a full day?" Apple claims that the new SE "lasts almost the same as the iPhone 8."

In the real world, it denotes that it'll give an average user a full day's charge. During multiple tests, it wasn't as durable as the iPhone 11's larger range, as the battery capacity in the SE is less, but it's good enough.

The fact that it can charge wirelessly, or using the fast charge function, remember that you will have to buy a new power adapter for it to work since the 18W is not included in the box, it means that you will be able to recharge quickly on the go anyway.

Does iPhone SE have good cameras?

- It has a 12-megapixel wide-angle, f / 1.8 aperture single rear camera
- 4K video at 60 fps, slow motion at 240 fps (at 1080p)
- Compatible portrait mode lighting effects
- No night mode

Unlike iPhone X, iPhone 11, and iPhone 11 Pro, iPhone SE only has a camera on the back. That means there is no optical zoom (it's digital-only), no ultra-wide-angle, no extra bells, and whistles.

It's the same sensor found on the original iPhone 8, but with several software enhancements to bring it to 2020 performance levels. And before you ask, it's not the iPhone XR's camera either.

With the new A13 Bionic processor, the iPhone SE can offer the full range of lighting effects in portrait mode, Smart HDR, and Quick Take Video (allowing you to press and hold to start a video recording).

You cannot use Portrait mode on anything other than people. It just won't work. But that shouldn't matter to most people unless you like taking photos of your dog or cat. Portrait mode also continues to have issues from time to time, especially with sparse hair and thin spectacle frames, which can fade, but overall it's very good.

The iPhone SE doesn't offer the Night Mode feature for taking photos in low-light conditions, and you don't get Deep Fusion, Apple's intelligent artificial intelligence that further enhances photos, such as it does on the iPhone 11 range. We miss night mode, especially since low-light images are still blurry at times.

The iPhone SE (2020) has to do with great power at a lower price. It is quite remarkable what this small iPhone offers. The smartphone will be incredibly attractive to all those iPhone 6, 6S, 7,

7S, and iPhone 8 users who want to upgrade, but don't want a physically bigger or more expensive phone.

Set Up iPhone SE (2020)

- First, you put your Nano-SIM in the bottom right corner of the iPhone SE in the designated slot.
- Hold the power button for a few seconds until your iPhone powers on and displays a screen with "Hello."
- Next, tap the home button.
- Swipe your screen to select your preferred language.
- After choosing your preferred language, you'll be required to select your country or region where you reside. Scroll down and make your selection. I choose "**United States**."
- Next, a screen with the caption "**Quick Start**" will pop up with instructions to either set up your device automatically or "Manually." If you want to set your iPhone, automatically follow the instructions on the screen. For this guide, we'll opt to select the option "**Set Up Manually**."

- When you're done with the above step, you'll be required to choose a Wi-Fi network to facilitate the setup. If there's no Wi-Fi, select the option "**Connect to Mac or PC**." To use a Wi-Fi network, select from the options displayed on your phone (make sure your Wi-Fi router is turned on).
- You'll be prompted to enter the Wi-Fi's password. Input the password to continue.
- After you've completed the above step, a "**Data & Privacy**" option will appear on the screen. Tap "**Continue**" to proceed.
- Next, a screen will appear, prompting you to set up "**Touch ID**." To set up Touch ID immediately, tap "**Continue**" to set up later tap "**Set Up Later in Settings**." I choose the second option. You'll learn how to set it up yourself later in this book.
- Another screen will pop up, prompting you to secure your device by setting a passcode. Tap "**Passcode Options**" to display your preferred type of passcode.
- Choose your passcode type from the options displayed or tap "**Don't Use Passcode**" if you don't want to set up passcode now.
- The "**Apps & Data**" screen will appear, asking your preferred method of sending your saved data to your iPhone. Make selection base on your preference and

follow prompt to retrieve your data. Choose "**Don't Transfer Apps & Data**."
- The next screen will require you to set up your "**Apple ID**," if you have one, enter it in the blank field and tap "**Next**" at the top left corner to proceed. If you don't have, tap on "**Forgot password or don't have an Apple ID**?"
- Next, the "**Terms & Conditions**" page will appear, touch "**Agree**" to proceed.
- An "**Express Settings**" screen; these settings entail the use of your personal details and other Apple Analytics. Tap "**Continue**" to proceed or tap "**Customize**" to control these settings.
- Next, a screen asks you how to get updates to appear; to automatically get updates such as iOS upgrades tap "**Continue**" to control or run the updates manually, tap "**Install Updates Manually**."
- You'll be required on the next screen whether to enable "**Location Services**" or not? Select "**Enable Location Services**" or "**Disable Location Services**."
- Next is the "**Apple Pay**" screen, select "**Continue**" to set up Apple Pay immediately or tap "**Set Up Later in Wallet**" to configure it later on.
- Next, a screen to set up "**Siri**" will appear, tap "**Continue**" to set up the feature now, or tap "**Set Up Later in Settings**" to set it up later on.

- Another screen will display prompting you to configure the settings for "**Screen Time**," to set it up now, tap '**Continue**," to do it some other time, select "**Set Up Later in Settings**."
- Next, the iPhone Analytics page will appear. To share your data with Apple, select "**Share with Apple**." To decline sharing your data with the company, select "**Don't Share**."
- An "App Analytics" screen, to share your data with the developers, select "**Share with App Developers**," to decline, tap "**Don't Share**."
- We're almost getting to the finish line here. A "True Tone Display" screen will appear, to see how the screen will look without it, tap "**See Without True Tone Display**" and the screen will respond. Tap "**Continue**" to continue.
- Next, the "**Appearance**" screen will pop up. Choose how your background will look like, switch between "**Light**" and "**Dark**" to see which one best suits you. Tap "**Continue**" to proceed.
- The "**Display Zoom**" page will appear, switch between "**Standard**" and "**Zoom**" to see which one best suits your taste; you'll learn how to change these settings later in this book too. Tap "**Continue.**"
- The next three screens that will appear are basically instructions screen with the label "**Go Home**," "**Switch Between Apps**"

and "**Quick Access Control**" respectively. Tap the "**Continue.**"
- Next, swipe up to view your home screen.

How to Set up Touch ID

You can easily unlock your Apple iPhone SE from standby by using the fingerprint scanner. Also, you can use it to authenticate purchases from the App Store, iTunes Store, and iBooks Store.

- Navigate to Settings on your iPhone SE.
- Move down and tap **Touch ID & Passcode**.
- If passcode has not been set, tap **Turn Passcode On**.
- Input a six-digit passcode.
- Re-enter the six-digit passcode.
- Touch **Add a Fingerprint**.
- Read the message and press the Home button to proceed.
- Lift and place your finger on the home button repetitively until the fingerprint turns red.
- Next, tap **Continue**.
- Finally, Touch ID has been set.

Restore from iCloud Backup

When you're initially setting up your iPhone for the first time, you'll get the prompt to restore from backup.

- When you get to the "**App & Data**" page, tap **Restore from iCloud Backup**.
- Enter the Apple ID and password you are using for iCloud, then tap **Next**.
- The terms of use will be displayed. Tap **Agree**.
- A list of backups stored in iCloud appears with the name of the device and the date the backup was taken. In addition to iPhone backup, you can also choose from backups of other devices such as iPad.
- When you select a backup, the settings will be restored.
- When restoration of settings is completed, and the home screen is displayed, restoration of apps, photos, ringtones, etc. will begin.

Turn On iCloud Backup

This is done automatically once a day as long as you set it. Key content is backed up, but not all.

iCloud can use up to 5GB for free. If there is not enough space, change the storage plan from the iPhone settings app.

- Open the **Settings** app
- Next, tap **your name** at the top of the display.
- Then tap **iCloud**.
- A list of iCloud functions will be displayed. Tap **iCloud Backup**.
- If iCloud Backup is off, turn it on.
- Turning on iCloud backup turns off automatic backup via iTunes
- When **iCloud Backup** is turned on, the backup via iTunes that is automatically performed when the iPhone is connected to the computer is turned off.
- Since iCloud backups and iTunes automatic backups cannot be used together, it is usually a good idea to use iCloud backups and regularly back up manually with iTunes.
- Tap **Create backup now** to start back up on the spot. A Wi-Fi environment is required, but it is not necessary to connect to a power source.
- The backup is complete when the message "**Creating backup**" disappears, and the time of the previous backup is displayed.

How to Reset iPhone

- From the home screen, tap **Settings > General**, then tap **Reset** at the bottom of the "**General**" screen.
- Tap **Erase all content and settings** to initialize iPhone.
- If you select **Reset All Settings**, the settings information such as mail and Wi-Fi will be reset, but the data (the contents of mail / message, photos, apps, etc.) will remain. If you have set a passcode, you will be prompted to enter it.
- After that, when you tap **Erase iPhone**, you will be asked: "**Do you really want to continue?**" Tap **Erase iPhone** again.
- Your iPhone initialization will starts.
- If you have not set a passcode, you will be asked for your Apple ID password before initialization.

How to Turn ON/OFF iPhone

- Go to **Settings** > **General** and scroll to the very bottom where you will see the Shutdown option.
- Click the **Shutdown option**. Drag the "**Slide to Power Off**" slider to the right to power off your iPhone.

- Alternatively, to get into the switch-off menu, you must hold down one of the two-volume buttons in addition to the side button (formerly the power button), and you will see a "**Slide to Power Off**" option. Drag it to the right to switch off your device.

How to Enable Emergency SOS

- Press and hold the Side button, and one of the Volume keys, so you basically squeeze both sides of the device.
- Continue holding until the **Emergency SOS** countdown appears on the screen. You can wait for the countdown to finish or to slide in to call emergency services immediately and notify your emergency contacts.

- If you do not want Emergency SOS to automatically call the emergency services. when the Side button is pressed, be sure to disable the "Auto Call" via **Settings > SOS Emergency > Disable Auto Call**.

How to Create a New Apple ID

- Open the **Settings** app.
- Click on Sign in to your iPhone at the upper part of the screen.
- Tap "**Don't have an Apple ID.**"
- Next, tap **Create Apple ID**.

- Enter your birthday, then tap "**Next**" at the top right of the screen.

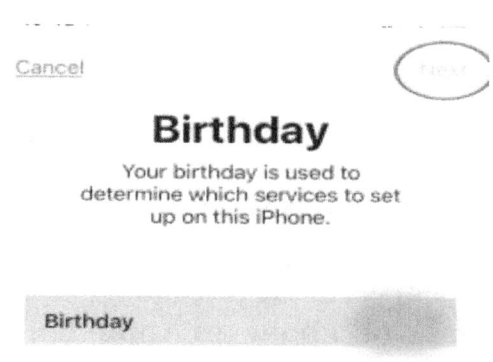

- Now enter your name and press "**Next**."

- Choose your "**existing email address**" or opt to "**get a free iCloud address**."

Email Address

Use your current email address

Get a free iCloud email address

- Input your email address and then click "**Next**.".
- Now create a password eight characters long and click "**Next**.". Your password will have to include at least one uppercase letter and at least one numerals to go through.
- You will receive a text message or call to confirm your identity, tap **Continue**.
- Agree to the terms and conditions.
- Enter your iPhone Passcode, if it has one.
- Choose whether you want a confirmation email sent to the email address you enter or different.
- Enter the verification code from your email to your iPhone.
- Tap **Merge**.

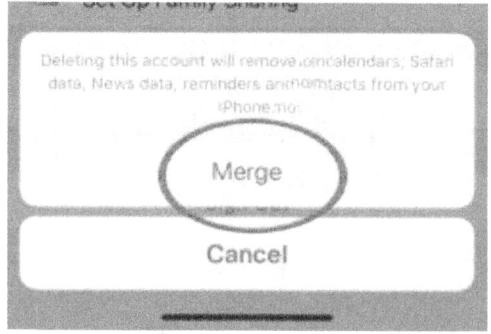

- That's all, from here you can adjust the payment and shipping information, set up iTunes and App Store, set up Family Sharing, and more.

Change Apple ID on the iPhone

- To log in with another Apple ID on your iOS device, navigate to the **Settings** app.
- Tap on **your name** above. At the top of the screen, you can view the Apple ID you're logged in with. Scroll down and touch "**Sign out**."
- Next, you will be required to enter your Apple ID and authorize your entry. In the following screen, you can select which information should be saved in the iCloud. To make a copy, you move the slider to the right; then, you tap again on "**Sign out**."
- Once your former Apple ID has been erased, you can now sign up again. Go into your settings and tap on "**Sign in to**

iPhone." Now you can enter the e-mail address and password for your other Apple ID.

Set Up Apple Pay

With Apple Pay, you can conveniently use contactless services in shops, such as the discount store, in restaurants, hotels, or at the gas station; pay with the iPhone, directly and without entering a PIN. This usually applies to amounts below a certain figure. For payments exceeding this maximum amount, it is usually necessary to enter the PIN for security reasons. By the way, if you use Apple Pay, you will not incur any costs. As with credit card payments, the respective dealer takes over the fees, so that the service is free for you.

Contactless payment is made possible by the NFC transmission standard, which allows the exchange of data over short distances. You can use Apple Pay wherever you see the following signs:

Configure Apple Pay on the iPhone
Method 1: Settings app

- Go to the **Settings** app.
- Touch "**Wallet & Apple Pay**"

- Next, tap "**Add Cards**."
- No matter which of the two ways you choose: After an info screen on the Apple Pay function, which you skip to "**Continue**" with a tip, you have the ability to scan your bank or credit card. The card number and your name will be taken over automatically. Alternatively, you can enter the card information manually.
- With a tip on "**Next**" in the top right, you jump to the next step. Your card will then be verified by the respective bank or card issuer. Once the verification is done, tap on "**Next,**" and you can use Apple Pay on your iPhone. Your card or cards are deposited directly in the Wallet app on the iPhone.
- You can add up to 12 cards. If you use multiple cards with Apple Pay, you can choose a preferred card by using the Wallet app. In the event that your default card is not accepted in a particular store, you can easily pay with another card via Apple Pay.

Method 2: Wallet app

- Go to **Wallet App** on your iPhone
- Tap the blue **Plus icon** in the top left corner of the home screen.
- Touch **Add Cards** to choose the card that you want to add.

CHAPTER TWO

Show Previews on the Lock Screen

- Launch the **Settings** app.
- Next, select "**Messages.**"
- Touch **Show previews**.
- In the next submenu, you can now choose one of three options: "**Always**," "**If Unlocked,**" or "**Never.**" Tap on "**Always,**" so that a small blue hook appears behind it. Then you can leave the settings again, and you will receive the messages directly as before without having to unlock the device.

How to Use a Wireless or USB Mouse

Make sure that Bluetooth is turned on and that you have not paired the mouse you want to use with another device.

- Open the **Settings** app.
- Scroll down and tap **Accessibility**.

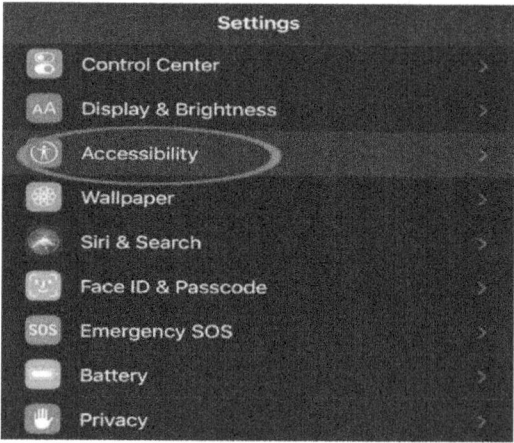

- Look under the "**Physical & Motor**" section and then click on "**Touch**."

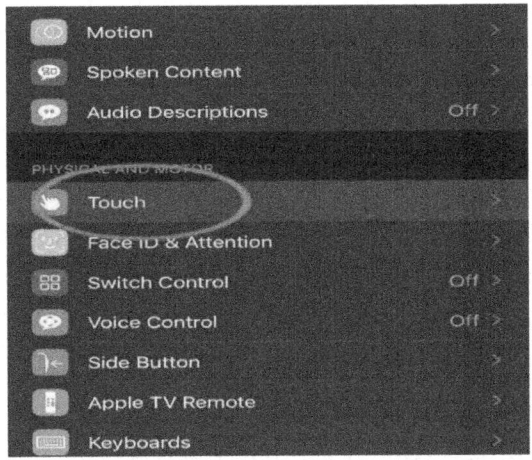

- In the menu toggle on "**Assistive Touch.**"

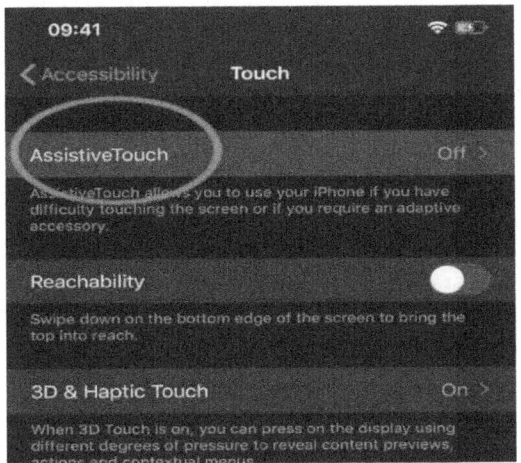

- And from here, you simply connect your mouse to your device. This should start immediately.

Tips for Using the Mouse

You can move the cursor the seconds you connect the mouse, but the cursor itself is a large, gray circle designed to imitate a fingerprint. The only way to change that is to make it bigger and change the color. It's not impossible to achieve the same precision you get with a desktop cursor, but that takes practice.

By default, the **AssistiveTouch** circular menu remains on the screen while **AssistiveTouch** is on, although you can move it across the screen with your finger. Usually, you also activate the AssistiveTouch menu by right-clicking. However, to hide the menu, you can go to "**Settings > Accessibility > Tap> AssistiveTouch**" and "**Always show menu**."

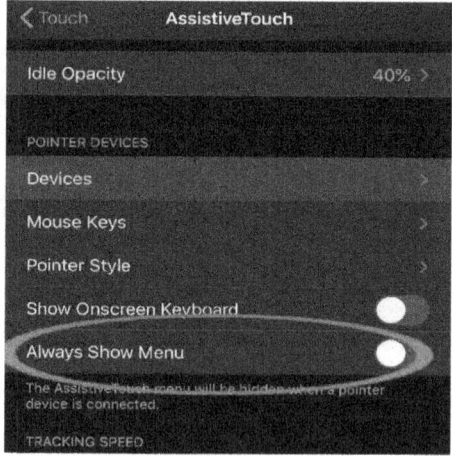

If you do not change the settings, the menu is always displayed when right-clicking.

Customize the Buttons on the Mouse

Go to **Settings** > **Utilities** > **Tap** > **AssistiveTouch** > **Pointing Devices**, and then select your connected mouse.

Customize AssistiveTouch

Assistive touch is a great accessibility feature in iOS devices. With this feature, you can perform arrays of gestures like pinch, multi-finger swipe, 3D touch, Pointing Devices, Mouse Keys etc. An important thing is while you've turned on the Assistive Touch, the iOS device at the time doesn't require pressing any physical button either the home button or the power and volume buttons. Double-tap the Assistive touch to display the App Switcher.

- Take a screenshot on iPhone without Side buttons by bringing up the Screenshot feature on the main menu of Assistive Touch.
- You can add gestures to the Assistive Touch Menu such as Home, Notification, Lock Screen, 3D Touch, and more. Tap the plus icon "+" to add the other settings to Assistive Touch.
- Launch the "**Settings**" app.
- Scroll down and select "**Accessibility**."

- Tap "**Touch**"
- Go to the "**AssistiveTouch**." Turn on **AssistiveTouch** to wake up on the home screen and use it like the Virtual Home button as well.
- Select "**Customize Top-Level Menu**."
- And if you don't like the customizations that you have made in Assistive Touch, then tap "**Reset**" on the same screen to revert the process.
- When you get back to **Touch Menu**, you will be allowed to set Custom Actions, like what will happen when you Single-Tap, Double-Tap and Long-Press the **Assistive Touch**. Open section one by one and make a selection.
- Note: All these options are available in Single-Tap, Double-Tap, and Long-Press custom actions in Assistive Touch.
- Keep in mind that when you "**Reset All Settings**," on iPhone, all the customized assistive touch settings will clear to default. You have to customize them again or else use them as it is.

CHAPTER THREE

Customize Text Message Tones

Each iPhone comes with many text tones. You can make one to be your default text tone. Each time you get a text message, the default tone will sound.

Change the default text tone by navigating through the process below:

- Go to the **Settings** app.
- Tap **Sounds & Haptics**.
- Tap **Text Tone**.
- Swipe to browse the list of text tones (you can utilize ringtones as text tones; they're on this screen, as well). Tap a tone to hear it play.
- When you've discovered the text tone you need to utilize, tap it to put a checkmark by it. Your decision is automatically saved, and that tone is set as your default.

Set Your Notification Preferences

You can pick whether to show an app notification's on the lock screen or if you'd only like it shown when your face has been recognized.

To customize this feature, go to **Settings > Notifications > Show Previews** to choose how content is or isn't shown on the lock screen, alternatively, go to **Settings > Notifications** to adjust the lock screen look.

Set Messages to Share Your Personalized Contact Data

New to iOS 13 is the option to create your very own contact photo and name to be displayed on other people's iPhone device. You can pick whether this is enabled for just contacts or everyone; however, they have the last say on whether they acknowledge your chosen information.

Tap **Settings > Messages > Share Name & Photo** where you can configure these and whom this automatically gets shared with.

Turn on Text, Call, and FaceTime forwarding

For calls, go to **Settings > Phone > Calls on Other Devices**, and toggle on the switch for the devices you'd like to get calls on. It's almost the same for messages and FaceTime, also. **Settings > Messages > Text Message Forwarding** gets you to similar toggles for messaging.

Filter Unknown Calls and Messages

You can have messages from unknown senders silenced and arranged into a separate list in your inbox for further review.

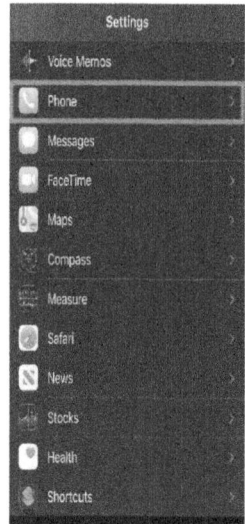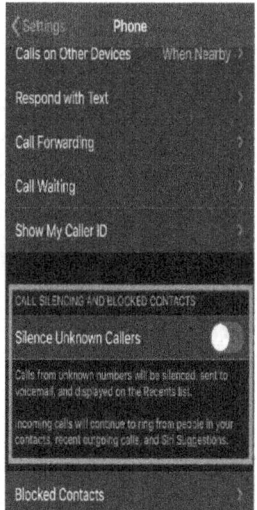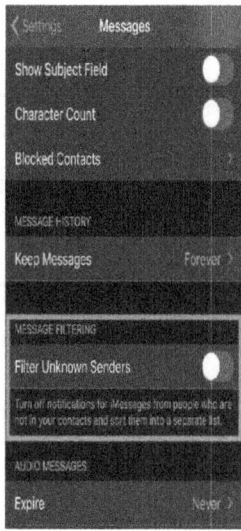

- For phone calls, go to **Settings > Phone > Silence Unknown Callers** and toggle the switch on to filter calls, or **Settings > Messages > Filter Unknown Senders** for message filtering.

Set Location Preferences

Apps

- To enable this feature go **to Settings.**

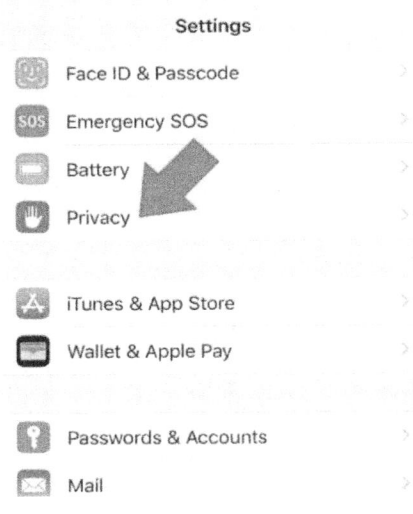

- Tap "**Privacy.**"

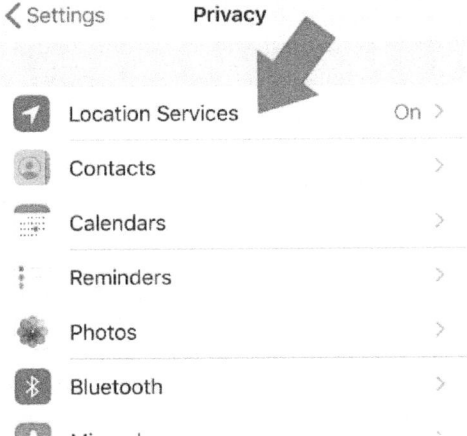

- Select "**Location Services**," to set a general rule for all apps, or go into each app and select "Never," "Always," while utilizing the app, or "ask next time."

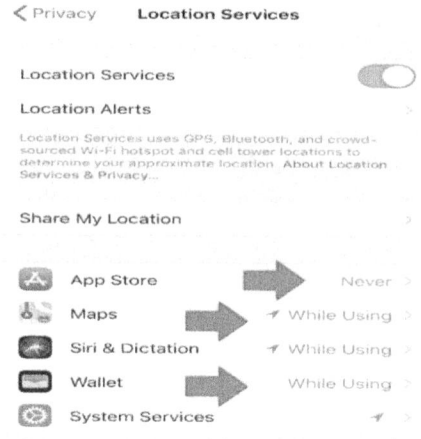

- The last option will prompt your iPhone to ask you each time an app requests to access your location data.

How to Enable iCloud Keychain on iPhone

You can use this feature to access your saved logins and passwords, credit card information, and personal details. First, you'll need to enable it.

- Open the **Settings** app
- Tap your **Apple ID banner**.
- Select **iCloud**.
- Scroll down and press **Keychain**.
- Turn on the **iCloud Keychain** switch.

- Input your Apple ID password if prompted.
- If this is your first time, you will be asked to create a password. You also have the option to verify it with another device. Next, if you resolve to complete your account, you'll be ready to store information more securely on your iPhone.

How to Access iCloud Keychain Passwords

- Open **Safari**
- In the menu bar, click "**Safari.**"
- Next, tap "**Preferences.**"
- Look for "**Passwords**" along the top. Here you'll see a list of passwords and login details for all web pages. Apple will notify you if you've recycled the same password on numerous web pages, and provide a swift link to change your password on a service's website.
- You can freely copy and paste the different usernames and passwords, and AirDrop them to other devices.

How to Activate Siri

- Head to **Settings**
- Tap **Siri & Search** > **Listen** to enable the feature.
- After you've enabled Siri, just say the command "**Hey Siri**" to activate the voice assistant.

Activate Siri with Side Button
To activate Siri, press and hold the Side button for a few seconds (two to three) will be okay.

How to Exit Siri
When you're done with Siri, and you want to exit, simply swipe up from the bottom of the screen or press the side button to return to the home screen.

Change Siri's language
- Go to **Settings**
- Swipe down and tap **Siri & Search**
- Select **Language**
- Pick a new language and tap **Change Language** to confirm your selection
- Tap the "**Hey Siri**" toggle on **Siri & Search** settings page to train Siri on the new language

CHAPTER FOUR

Change iPhone's Language

- On the Home screen, go to **Settings**.
- Next, tap **General**.

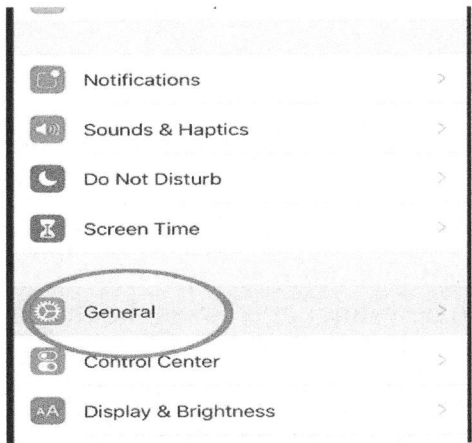

- Scroll down and select **Language & Region**.

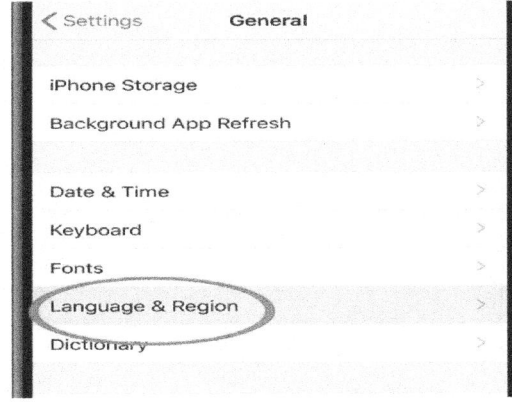

- On the following screen, choose "**iPhone Language**."

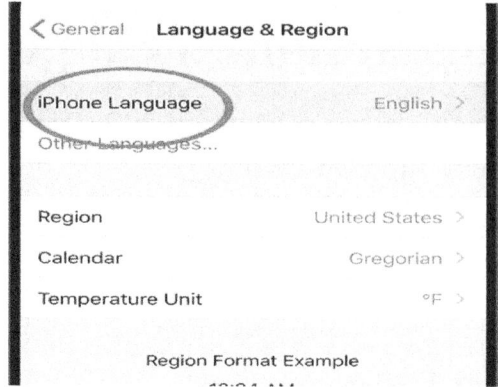

- Select your language from the rundown.
- A notification will require you to confirm the new language. Press the first option.
- After your iPhone updates the preferred language, it should automatically be showing the language you choose.

How to Scan Documents in the Files App

- Open the **Files app**, select the **Browse** tab, tap on the three-dot icon in the top-right corner, then **Scan Documents**.
- Hold your device over the document you want to scan, and it should automatically capture the page.
- You can scan multiple pages into one PDF file and then save it to iCloud or import it into another app once you're done.

How to Use iMessage Search

- To check it out, open the **Messages app**, swipe down to display the search field and type.
- Next, scamp through your past messages and make your desired decision.

Share Photos Without Location Information

- To see how this works, select an image(s) you want to share in the Photos app, then touch on **Options** at the top of the screen and turn off **Location** under the part labeled "**Include**."

Remove App Size Limitations on Cellular Data

Go to **Settings > iTunes & App Store > App Downloads** to get rid of the limit or have the App Store ask you if you want to download any apps over 200MB.

How to Take Long Screenshots of Websites

With this feature you no longer have to take multiple screenshots of a webpage in order to capture the text of an article, iOS 13's screenshot tool has a new tactic.

- Launch Safari and visit any website you want to take a screenshot.
- Next, take just one screenshot of the website and instantly tap on the thumbnail preview.

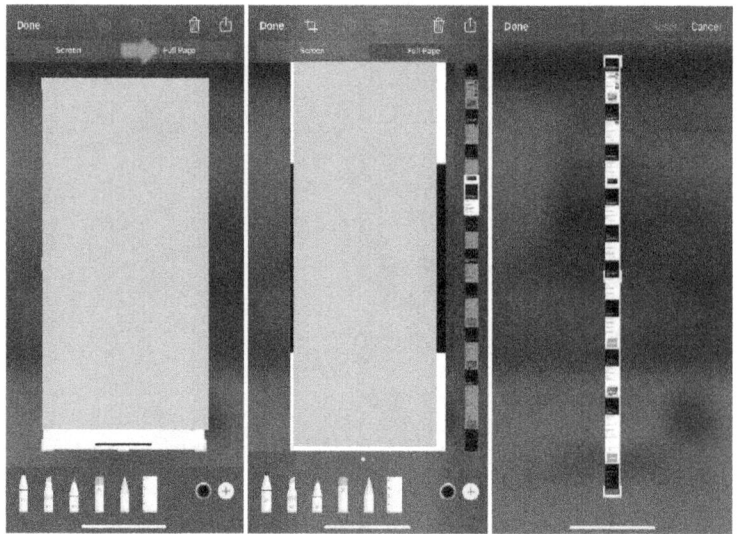

- Above the screenshot, there are two options: **Screen** and **Full Page**.
- Selecting **Full Page** will turn the entirety of the webpage you're viewing into a PDF file that you can then crop, annotate and save to the Files app.

Customize Notification Centre

- Go to **Settings**
- Select **Notifications**.

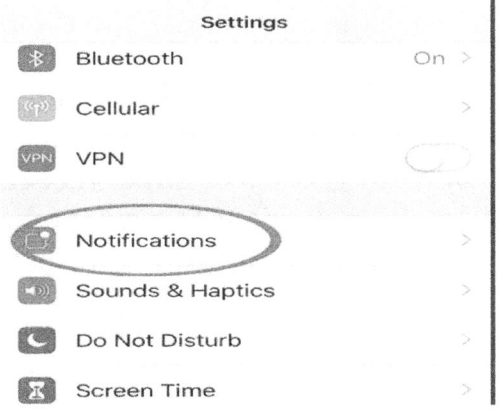

- Touch **Show Previews** at the upper part of the Notifications screen.
- Choose "**Always**," "**When**," "**Unlocked**," or "**Never**" and tap "**Back**" at the top of the screen to go back to the Notifications screen.

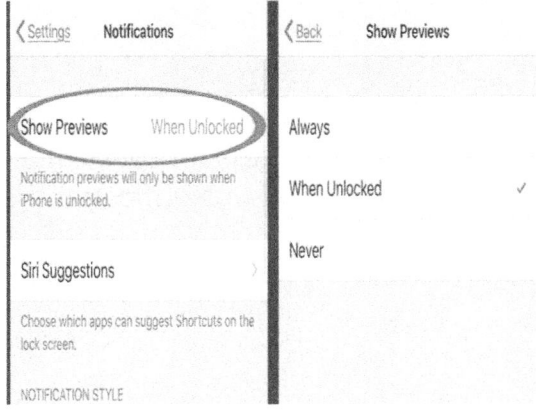

- Touch one or more of the apps on the display.
- Push the slider next to **Allow Notifications** to the **ON** position.

43

- Touch the circle under **Notification Center** to check it, and notifications from the app begin to display in the **Notification Center**. Alternatively, you can also select **Lock Screen** if you want notifications to appear on your lock screen and **Banner** if you want them to appear at the top of the screen.

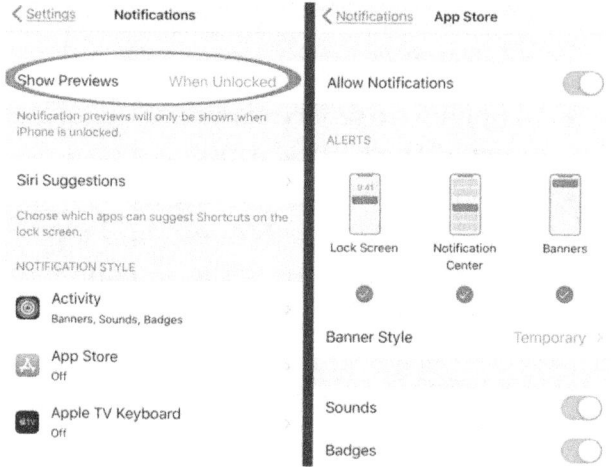

- Repeat this process for every other app you wish to post to Notification Center.

How to Switch Apps

- Touch your finger to the gesture area at the bottom of the iPhone SE display.
- Swipe from left to right to go to the former app.
- To return to the next app, swipe from right to left.
- Note, in the event that you stop or get interrupted, the last app you were on turns into the recent app so you can just swipe back from it, not forward anymore.

Display Multitasking Quick App Switcher

- Touch your finger to the gesture area at the bottom of the iPhone SE display.
- Swipe up slightly. (Try not to flick. Simply keep your finger on the screen until you get a short far up, the pull away.)

Force Quit Apps

- Touch your finger to the gesture area at the extreme bottom of the iPhone SE display.
- Swipe up slightly.
- Pause. Try not to lift your finger up right away. (That will take you Home.)
- Lift up your finger.
- Swipe up on an app card. Boom! It's gone.
- When you're in a killing mode, you can remove as many apps as you wish.

How to Access Reachability Mode

- Open **Settings** from the Home screen.
- Tap on **General**.
- Tap on **Accessibility**.
- Switch **Reachability** to ON.

How to Access Control Center

- Touch your finger to the gesture area at the extreme bottom of the iPhone SE display.
- Swipe down.
- Once more, you can even swipe down from the top right of **Reachability** to access **Control Center**.

CHAPTER FIVE

Set Up Monthly Cycle Data

- Launch **Health App** on your iPhone. Under the **Browse** tab, select the **Cycle Tracking** option from the rundown.

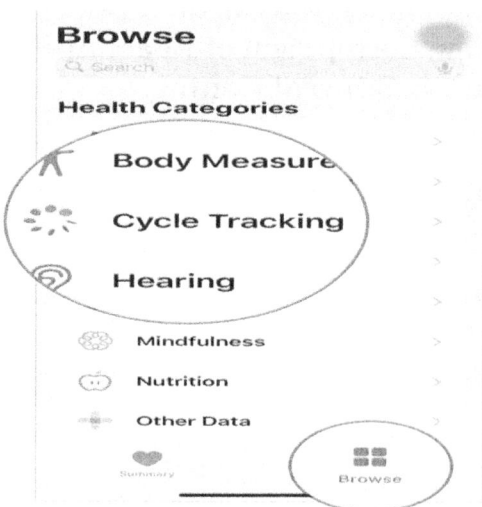

- Next, tap on **Get Started,** and now you'll be asked with specific questions, for example, when did your former period start? How long does your period normally last? How long is your regular cycle? And so forth. Enter every one of the information you know and tap on "**Next**" or tap on "**I Don't Know**" to continue. This will set up essential monthly cycle information on your iPhone.

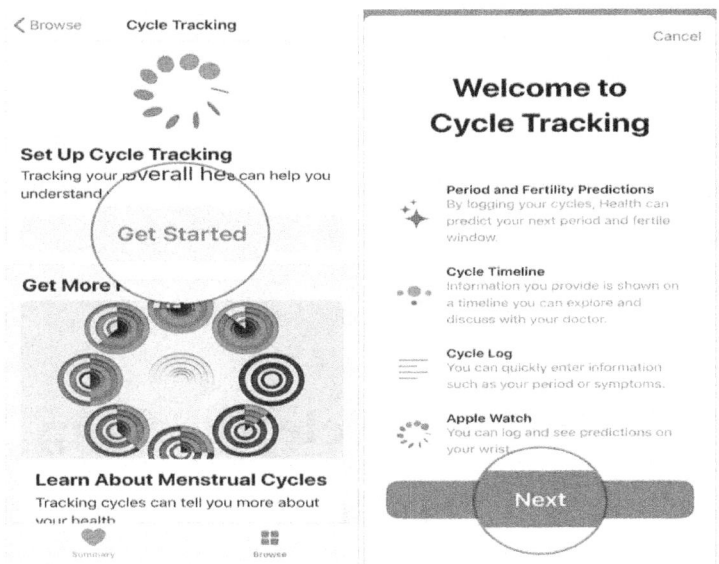

- If you need to edit the period length, just tap on **Options** directly beside **Cycle Log** and adjust the **period length** according to your cycle.

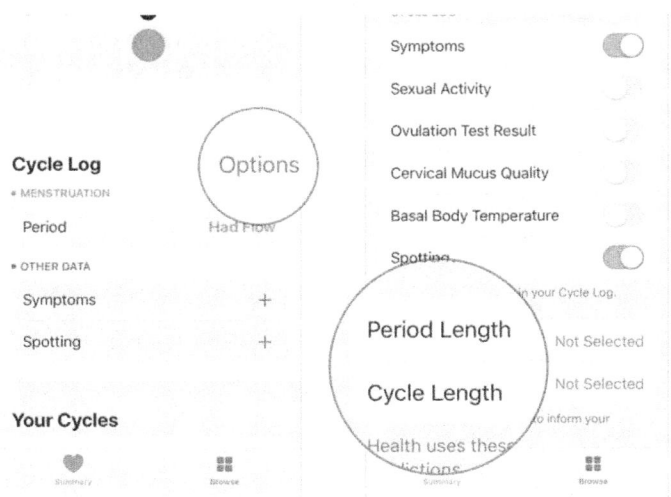

Make sure that every information is accurate as this will be used by the Health App to predict fertility schedule and period predictions. However, you can change the information as the month passes on the grounds that not all cycle is constant.

Customize Cycle Tracking Options

- Launch the **Health App** and head over to the **Cycle Tracking** option by scrolling down. Tap on **Options** directly beside **Cycle Log**.

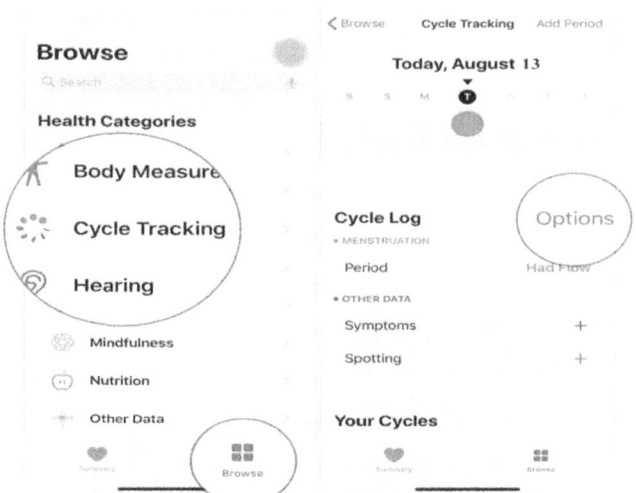

- Flip the Symptoms switch to ON and see the rundown of symptoms. Tap on the symptoms you're experiencing during your periods.

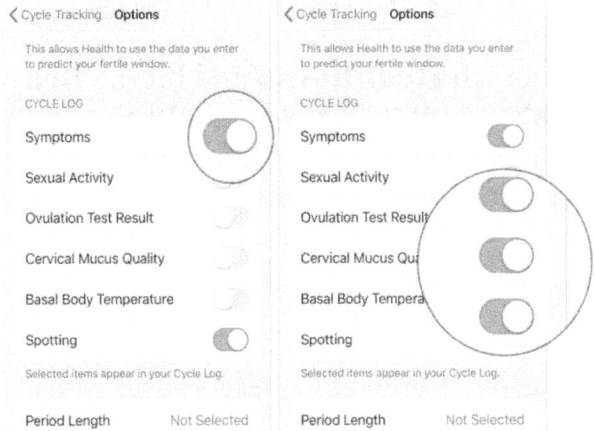

- Switch ON the **Ovulation Test Results** so as to see your logged ovulation test outcomes.
- Switch on options, for example, Cervical Mucus Quality, Basal Body Temperature, and Spotting to view the results.

This would give you a total idea with respect to your menstruation cycle and fertility, also if you want to give birth. Keep in mind these are simply predictions dependent on the information you enter in Cycle Tracking. It's constantly prescribed to consult a doctor before you decide on anything.

Receive Period Predictions and Notifications

- Launch **Health App** and hit the **Browse** tab to find the **Cycle Tracking** option.
- Tap on **Options,** which is directly beside **Cycle Log**.

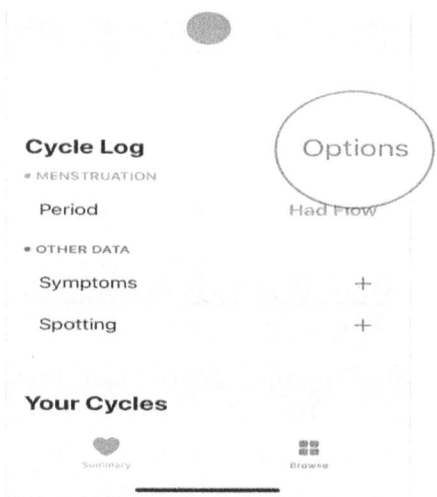

- Next, Toggle ON **Period Prediction** option to make a period prediction schedule for a two-month and Toggle ON **Period Notification** option to get updates to save your day by day information and get updates on your upcoming period.

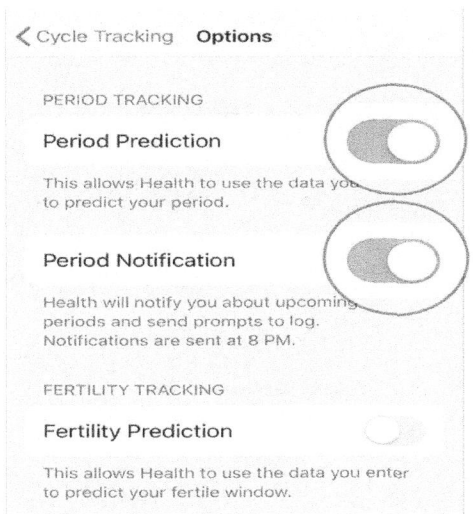

- The period prediction is one of the amazing highlights of Cycle Tracking in the Health app in iOS 13. Base on the first date of the period you entered, it'll establish a two-month schedule to predict in the next two months' your period time frame. This may be correct, yet sometimes it might go wrong too, as it's only a prediction all things considered.

Set Up Fertility Predictions and Notifications

- Launch the **Health App** and tap on the Browse tab
- Tap on the **Cycle Tracking** option.

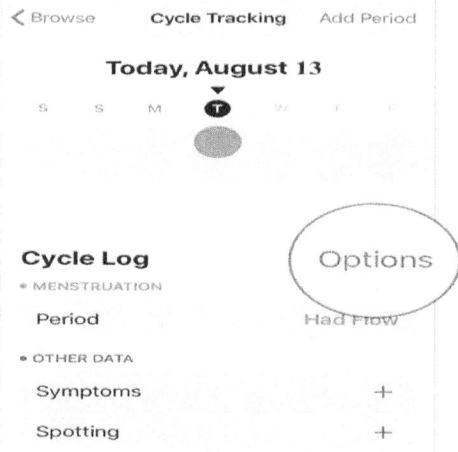

- Next, tap on **Options,** which is on the right side of **Cycle Log**.

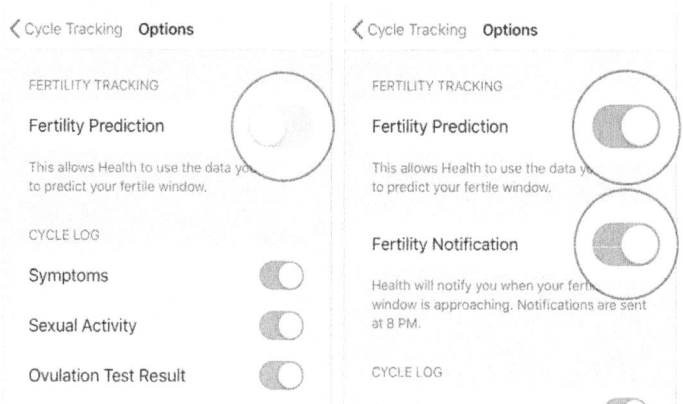

- In the fertility tracking segment, turn on **Fertility Prediction** and **Fertility Notification** to create a three-week schedule of next fertility and to get notifications about your next fertility window.

Manage Menstruation Flow

- Open **Health App**, go to the **Browse** tab, and tap on **Cycle Tracking** from the rundown.
- Tap on **Day** from the top and then tap on **Flow Level**.
- Note: Tap on **Add Period** from the top right corner if you have not logged your period date yet and select the date to begin.
- Next, select the flow level from the given options, for example, light, medium, heavy, unspecified (if you're not certain) or "**None**" and then tap on "**Done!**"
- Continue to do this until your period exists. This would help the app to be exact while predicting the period schedule and fertility frame. If you haven't included the previous month's period information, add it to get period calendar predictions now!

Add Cycle Symptoms to Cycle Tracking

- Open the **Health App** and then tap on the **Browse** tab
- Touch on the **Cycle Tracking** option.
- Tap on '+' icon next to Symptoms from other data section.
- Next, select the symptoms, for example, Headache, Lower Back Pain, and so forth, whichever you're encountering right now in the Cycle Tracking app. Tap on "**Done**" once you have selected these symptoms.

Remove Cycle Tracking Data

- Go to the **Cycle Tracking** option in the **Health App**.
- Tap on **View Cycle Tracking Items** from the bottom of the **Cycle Tracking** summary.
- Next, select the section or category log, for instance, **Cycle Tracking Symptoms**. After this, scroll down to bottom and tap on **Show All Data**.
- Tap on Edit at the upper right corner of the display

- Next, tap on **Remove Button** (red dot with a minus image inside)
- Finally, tap on **Delete** and afterward tap on "**Done**."

Disable True Tone Display

True Tone is a feature that automatically adjusts the white balance of your iPhone's display to correct for changes in ambient light conditions.

- Open the **Settings** app on your iPhone.
- Tap **Display & Brightness**.
- Toggle the True Tone switch to off.

How to Enable/Disable Tap to Wake

- Go to **Settings**
- Touch **General**
- Tap **Accessibility**
- Next, touch **Tap to Wake**.

- Toggle on or off the feature base on preference.

Set Up Haptic Touch

Haptic Touch is Apple's name for touching and holding your finger on the screen.

- Go to **Settings**
- Select **Accessibility**
- Choose **Touch**
- Finally, tap **Haptic Touch**
- Choose **Fast** or **Slow**
- To test the feature, touch the flower or flashlight icon under the **Touch duration test**.

How to Use Sign In with Apple Feature

Sign in with Apple is the company's new sign-in option that will act as an alternative to creating custom log-ins for individual sites, or logging into them with Google or Twitter credentials. It's important for three reasons: The two-factor authentication makes it secure, it can save people from juggling complicated passwords, and Apple says it limits private data sharing with third parties.

- Open an app for the first time and click on the "**Sign in with Apple**" option, then confirm who you are with your phone's passcode or Touch ID.

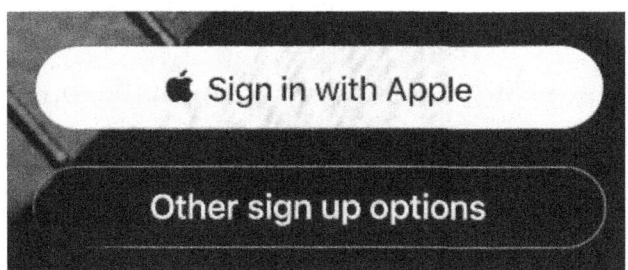

- There's no inventing another complicated password you'll have to remember or store in a password manager. You'll stay logged in on that device, and it works across other devices and on the Web. Developers can even add it to their Android apps.

- When you sign in with your Apple ID and select "**Private Email**," Apple creates a user-specific email address and forwards it to your original email address. You can share your email address only with trusted apps and websites.

Share Your Location Using the Apple Map

It's easy to share your location with friends and family directly from the Apple Map app via the steps below.

- Launch the Maps app on the Home screen.
- Tap the location arrow in the top right corner to ensure your location is precise.
- Touch the blue dot that denotes your current location.
- Next, click on **Share My Location**.
- In the sharing pane, choose how to share your location, either via Messages, Mail, and others.
- In the "**To**" text box, input the recipient or address details and then send the message.

CHAPTER SIX

How to Use Memoji Feature

- Open iMessage on your iPhone and tap on create a new message icon.

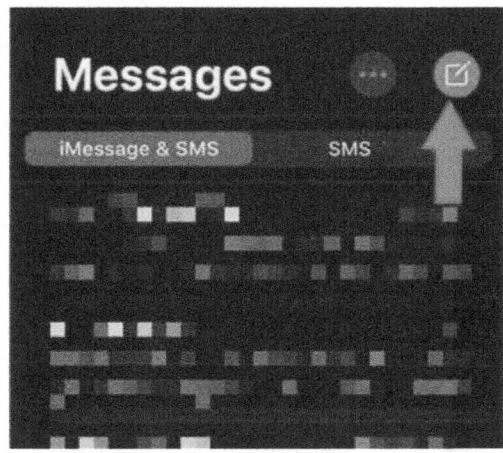

- Once it launches, you should see a new Memoji icon staring at you.

- Tap on it to launch Memoji, and you will be greeted with the "+" icon.

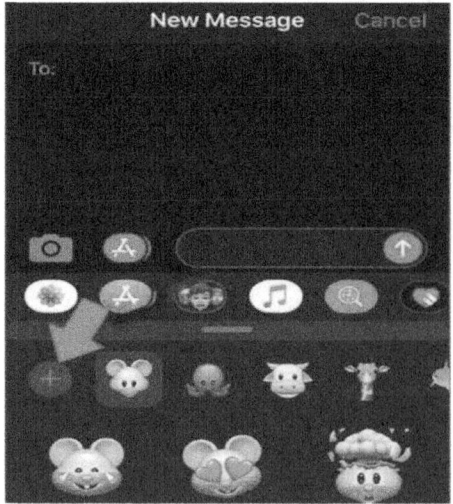

- Tap on that to begin creating your Memoji, which is nothing but your digital avatar. You will now begin customizing Memoji.

How to Create Memoji

- Choose from a variety of skin tones here. There is a slider to help you pan and select one. Select the freckles option.

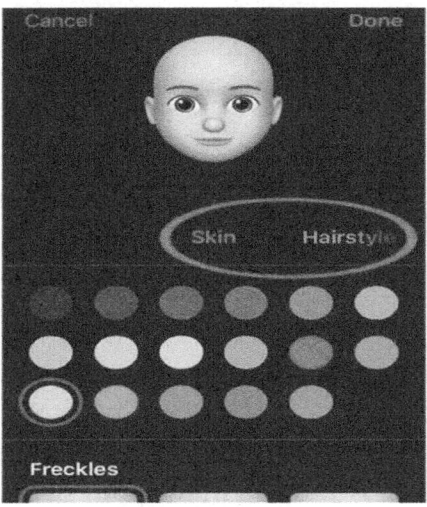

- Pick a hairstyle. To find hairstyles for men/boys, scroll a little more. Apple has decided not to go the gender way, so everything is available on the same screen. Continue with choosing your head and nose shape. Then select appropriate eyebrows for your Memoji.
- You can also cycle between appropriate nose shape, and also pick ear piercings if you have any or just want to use them on the Memoji. Finally, there are eye and headwear options to complete the look.

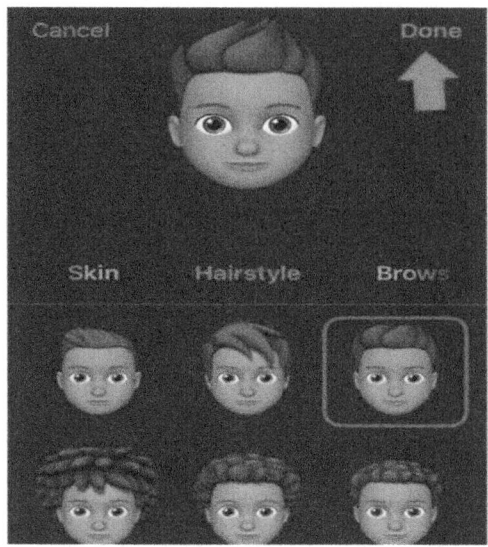

- Tap on "**Done**" to save. Do not go back at any point during the process because you will have to begin from scratch. That said, it doesn't take more than a few moments either. After you make your Memoji, iOS 13 will create a bunch of stickers automatically.

Edit, Delete or Create Another Memoji

- Go back to iMessages and either start a new conversation or enter an existing one. Instead of the "+" icon, you will see a menu icon. Tap on it to find some new options.

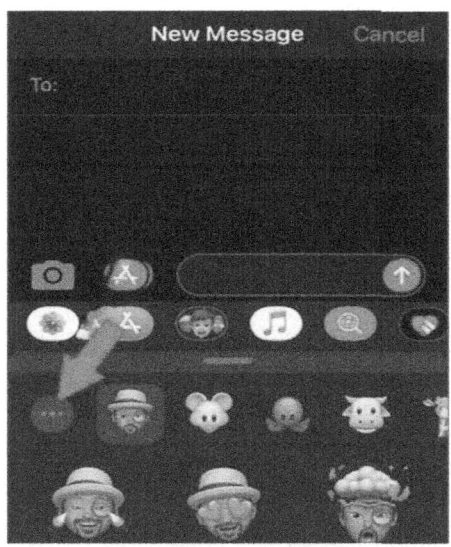

- Tap on the **New Memoji** button to begin the process all over again.

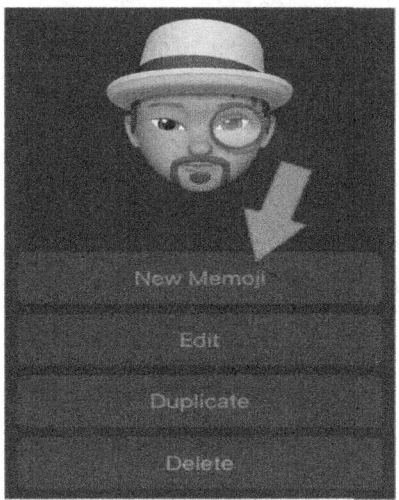

- Tap on the **Edit** button to change features of the current or selected Memoji. Finally, tap on the **Delete** option to delete the Memoji.

- Tap on the **Duplicate** button to create the exact same Memoji, and then quickly change certain features to create a new one on the fly.
- Every new Memoji you create will be in the gallery with its respective set of stickers. Pretty fun.

How to Remove Memoji Option

- Open a new message or reply to an old one, and tap on **More**.

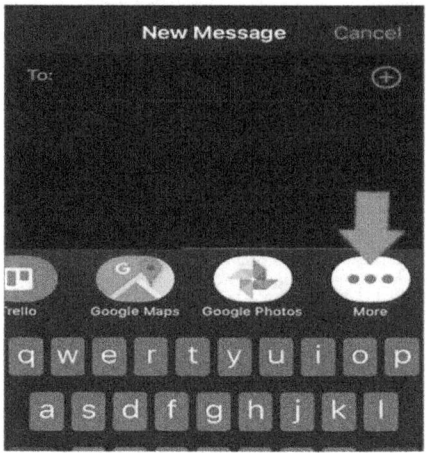

- You will then select **Edit**.

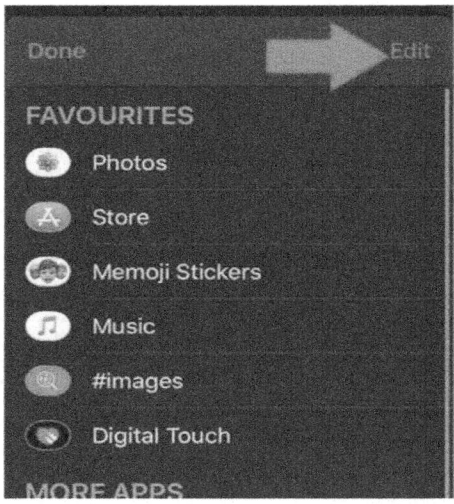

- Tap on the "-" icon next to the Memoji button to remove it from the list.

- You can add and remove other features similarly.

How to Use Siri Shortcuts

Siri Shortcuts allows you to do regular tasks rapidly, and with the apps, you utilize the most with only a tap or by asking Siri. Siri learns your routines across your apps. Siri then recommends a simple method to perform common tasks on the Lock screen or in Search. For instance, if you request news flash consistently on an app, Siri may recommend your preferred news.

- To utilize a Siri Suggestion, simply tap it on the lock screen. On the other hand, swipe down from the center of your screen to show **Search**; at that point, tap the **Siri Suggestion**.

Add Shortcuts to Siri

You can likewise run any shortcut by asking Siri. Search for the "**Add to Siri**" button in your most-used apps and tap to include with your very own expression or then again go to **Settings** to find all shortcuts accessible on your iPhone.

Shortcuts that require an app to open on your iPhone won't take a shot at HomePod and Apple Watch.

Add Shortcut from a third-party App

- Launch the third-party app and tap **Add to Siri**.

- Tap (red icon). At that point, record a personal catchphrase that you'll say to Siri to run the shortcut. Ensure that you record an easy expression that you'll recall.

- Tap "**Done**."

Add Shortcut from Settings

- Go to **Settings** > **Siri & Search**.

- You'll see three proposed shortcuts. Tap **All Shortcuts** to see more actions from various apps.
- Tap **Plus**.

- To record a personal expression, tap (red icon). Attempt to record an easy expression that you'll recall.
- Tap "**Done.**"

Delete a shortcut or change the phrase

- Head to **Settings > Siri & Search** and touch My Shortcuts.
- To change the expression for the shortcut, tap the shortcut, at that point, tap **Re-Record Phrase**.
- To erase a shortcut, swipe left over the shortcut and then tap **Delete**. Alternatively, tap the shortcut and tap **Delete Shortcut**.

How to Set Screen Time

- Tap the "**Settings**" app.
- Select "**Screen Time**."
- Tap "**Turn on screen time**."
- Touch "**Continue**."
- Tap "**This is an iPhone for children**."
- Tap "**Done**"
- Next, tap "**Done.**"
- Tap "**Continue**."
- Enter the passcode.
- Input the passcode again.

Restrict Functions of Apps

You can restrict the use of various apps by following the settings below.

- Launch the "**Settings**" app.
- Tap "**Screen Time**."
- Touch "**Content & Privacy Restrictions**."
- Enter the screen time passcode.
- Tap "**Allowed App**."
- Turn off apps you want to restrict.
- When you check the home screen, the app icon disappears, and usage is restricted.

Restrict Use of Contents

- Tap the "**Settings**" app.
- Tap "**Screen Time**."

- Tap "**Content & Privacy Restrictions**".
- Enter the screen time passcode.
- Tap "**Content Restriction**."
- Tap "**App**."
- Set the App rate that is allowed to use, and the setting is complete.

Restrict Access to Websites
- Tap the "**Settings**" app.
- Tap "**Screen Time**."
- Tap "**Content & Privacy Restrictions**".
- Enter the screen time passcode.
- Tap "**Content Restriction**."
- Tap "**Web Content**."
- Select one of the following settings depending on the intensity you want to limit.
- Tap "**Restrict adult website**."
- Tap "**Only allowed websites**."
- Always tap the "**Add Web Site**" permission.
- Enter the URL and tap, "**Done**."
- Allowed websites are added to "**Always Allowed**."

Change Screen Brightness

- Go to the **Settings** app
- Choose "**Screen Display & Brightness**"
- Adjust the brightness by moving the slider displayed in "**Brightness**" left or right

Turn on Automatic Brightness Adjustment

- Launch the **Settings** app on your iPhone
- Go to "**Accessibility**"
- Select "**Screen Display & Text Size**"
- Turn "**automatic brightness adjustment**" on/off.

Shorten Automatic Lock

- Launch the **Settings** app on your iPhone
- Go to "**Screen Display & Brightness**"
- Select "**Auto Lock**"
- Set the time until automatic lock. The display does not go dark while looking at the screen.

CHAPTER SEVEN

How to Change Wallpaper

- Launch the **Settings** app on your iPhone
- Go to **"Wallpaper"**
- Select **"Select wallpaper."**
- Select the photo or image you want to set as wallpaper
- At the lower right of the phone, tap **"Settings."**
- Tap **Set to locked screen / Set to home screen / Set for both**.

Add Widget to Display the Battery Level as a Percentage

- Pair with a Bluetooth device such as AirPods, Apple Watch, or wireless earphone
- On the first page of your phone's home screen, slide left to access **"Today's View."**
- Tap "**Edit**"

- Tap **"+"** next to **"Battery"** to add a battery widget.

How to Control Offload Unused Apps

Remove unused apps on your device to free up storage space. In addition to automatically removing apps when the remaining storage capacity is low, you can also remove any apps manually.

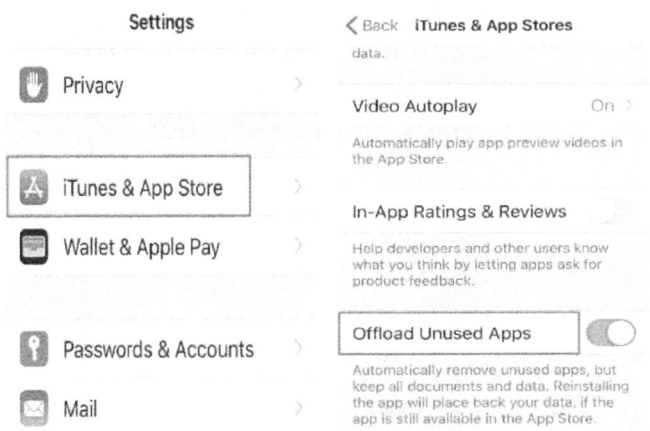

- By selecting **"iTunes Store & App Store"** from **"Settings"** on your iPhone and turning on **"Offload Unused Apps,"** apps that are not in use are automatically used when the iPhone storage capacity is low will be removed.

Restrict Offload Unused Apps

- From the **Settings** app, tap **Screen Time**.
- Next, tap to turn on **Content & Privacy Restrictions**.
- Then, directly underneath, tap **iTunes & App Store Purchases**.
- Tap **Deleting Apps**.
- Follow the arrow to the next screen and touch **Don't Allow**.
- With that control set, no one can delete apps from your phone from now on unless you explicitly lift the restriction.

Move Home Screen Apps

- First, press and hold any icon.
- Then, a thumbprint will be displayed on the upper left of the icon, as shown in the image below, and it will move like a wave.
- The icon can now be moved.
- Then press the icon you want to move with your finger.

- Move your finger to the place you want to move without releasing your finger.
- By the way, you can't place app icons anywhere on your iPhone or iPad, like Android smartphones.
- There may be cases where you can use unofficial app icons, but basically, app icons are arranged in order from the top.

Moving Apps to Another Page

Next, I will explain how to move to another page when moving the icon.

- Long press the app
- A thumbprint appears on all icons
- Keep pressing the icon you want to move with your finger
- Move to the page you want to move
- Switch to the page you want to move and place an icon.

Create a Folder on the Home Screen

- First, press and hold the icon.
- To delete, move, or create a folder, you must first press and hold the icon, the thumbprint is displayed, and the icon is wavy.
- You can now edit the home screen icons.
- First, tap the icons you want to organize into a folder.
- Move the icons in the previous chapter so that they overlap the icons you want to put together in the same folder.
- Then, a folder is automatically created.
- Move and place the icon in the folder as it is.

Reset Icon Layout on Home Screen

- Go to **Settings** app
- Tap **General**
- Tap **Reset Home Screen Layout.**

Enable Location Services on Find My App

To use the Find My app, you have to enable location services on your iPhone. The flows below will guide you on that.

- Go to **Settings**
- Tap **Privacy**.
- Select **Location Services**.
- Toggle on **Location Services**.

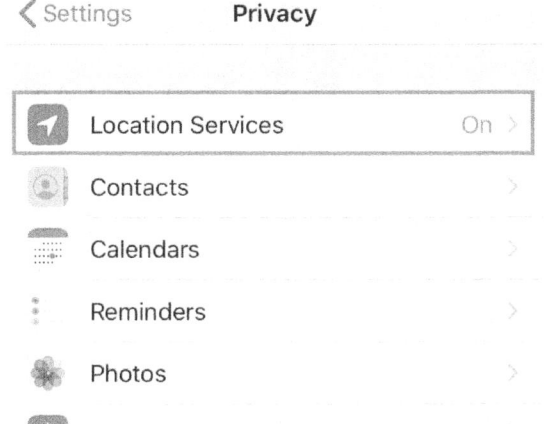

- If you would like to share your location with others, you can do that from this area of the Settings as well by tapping **Share My Location** and turning on the toggle on the next screen.

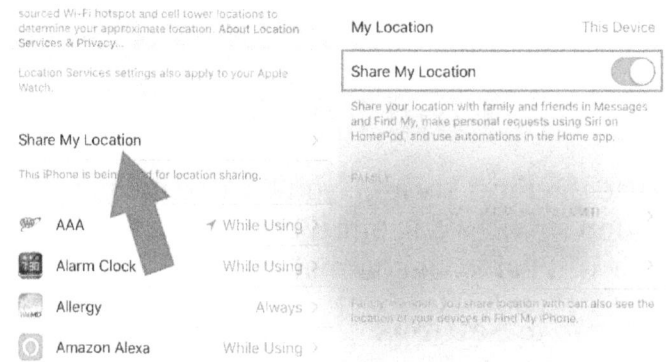

Another way to do this is demonstrated below;

- Go to **Settings**
- Touch your **Apple ID** at the top
- Click on "**Find My**"
- Next, turn on **Share My Location**.

Locate Family/Friends on Find My App

If you need to locate someone who has shared their location with you, it's easy and simple.

- Launch "Find My" app
- Touch People at the bottom and touch the person on your list. You'll then view their location on the map.
- You also have preferences to Contact them, get Directions to their spot, add Notifications, and lots of other kinds of stuff.

Share Your Location via Find My App

- To share your location, launch Find My and tap "**Me**" at the bottom. Ensure the toggle is activated for Share My Location.

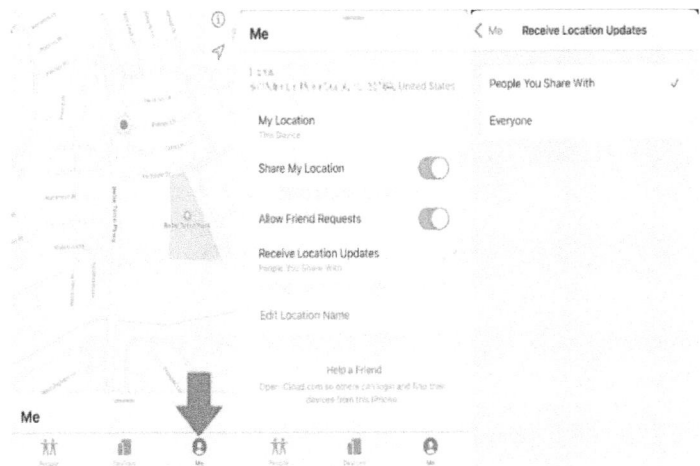

- You have a preference also to **Allow Friend Requests**, choose to **Receive Location Updates** with everyone or only people you share with, and **Edit Location Name**.

Enable Offline Finding via Find My App

- Launch the "Find My" app and choose **Devices** at the bottom. You'll see each of your devices on the list at the bottom, along with their locations on the map.

- Tap to select a particular device and then **Play Sound** to help you find it or get **Directions** to it. You can also "**Mark As Lost**" and get **Notifications** when the device is found. If you deem it fit, you can remotely **Erase This Device**.

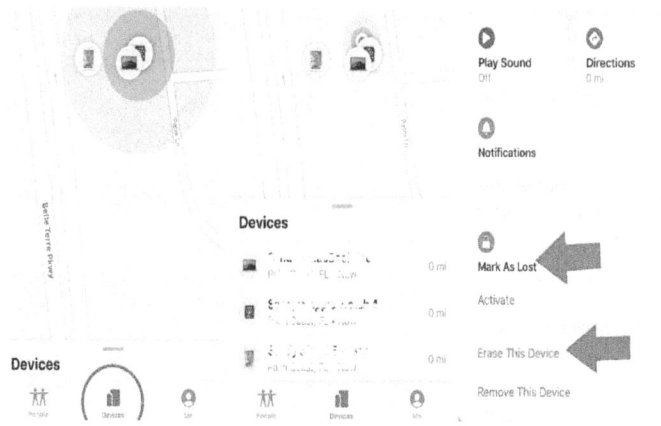

- You can also use this feature to find iOS devices belonging to others who've shared their location with you. For instance, if your friend lost their device, their devices will show up in the list for you to choose and locate the same way you locate yours.

Verify Offline Finding is Turned On

- Open the **Settings** app and tap your name up top to view your Apple ID settings.
- Touch "**Find My**" option.
- Next, tap "**Find My iPhone**."

- On the page that pops up, make sure "**Enable Offline Finding**" is turned on.

How to Create a New Reminder

- Launch the "**Reminder**" app and touch "**Add list**" at the bottom right corner of the screen. Previously "**Reminders**" were just a list of created lists, but in the new version, the reminders are automatically organized to "**Today**" or "**Flag**" according to the set contents.
- Next, register the name and appearance of the list. You can choose various colors and icons according to the content. After setting, tap "**Done**" at the top right of the screen. The newly created list will be added to "**My List**," so select it.
- Tap "**New Reminder**" at the bottom left of the screen and enter the name of the reminder. At this time, you can set the date and time to receive notifications by tapping the icon displayed on the keyboard. You can also add flags, photos, and scanned documents.

Receive Notification When Sending Message via Reminder App

- To set it, first tap the "**i**" icon displayed at the right end of the reminder, then tap "**Notify when sending a message**."
- Next, select the contact of the other party. Send a message to the person you choose here to receive a reminder notification.
- Try sending a message to the person you selected. If you forget the event and send a casual message, you will receive a reminder reminding you of the event.

Remove Reminder

- The first is to select only the items you want to delete and delete them manually. Open the list and swipe left on the reminder you want to erase. When "**Delete**" appears, swipe further to the left. Only one event has been deleted.
- The second method is to delete the list itself. Open the list and tap "**Delete List**" at the top right of the screen. Tap "**Delete**" again to delete the list itself. Use it when you have achieved all of your goals.

Creating Grouped Lists via Reminder App

- First, you can tap "**Edit**" in the top right, then "**Add Group**" in the bottom left. That will prompt the **New Group** modal to open, but before we get to that, let's go over the second way to initiate a new grouping.
- Second, press-and-hold on one of your lists to catch it, drag it above another list that you want it grouped with, then drop it when the bottom list is highlighted. The **New Group** modal should open.
- You can only create grouped lists in iCloud, not third-party services. So if you have a Yahoo or Outlook section with lists in it you want to consolidate, it will have to wait until those services support it. Additionally, you cannot drag one list from one service over to a list that's in iCloud; lists stay put in their own accounts.
- Either way, in the **New Group** modal, choose a name for your lists group. After, you can view the lists that are included in the group via the "**Include**" menu item. There, you can remove some of the lists from the group (hit the red minus button) or other lists you already have (the green plus).
- If you want to change the order of your included lists, hold down on the three-bar icon on the right of a list and drag it up or

down to where you want it. When you're all set, tap "**Create**" to finish.

Add New Subtasks to Reminder

- So either create a "**New Reminder**" to be the parent or tap on a reminder in the list already that you want to be the parent. Next, tap on its information (*i*) icon to open its **Details** modal view. Tap on "**Subtasks**" near the bottom, then "**Add Reminder**" for each subtask you want to create.
- To make sure newly added subtasks are saved, hit the "**return**" or "**enter**" key on the keyboard or hit "**Add Reminder**" again after typing one out. That will pop you into a new bubble for the next subtask to add.
- If you add a subtask you didn't want, edit it to something else or short-swipe left on it and hit "**Delete**," or long-swipe left to remove it automatically. When no more subtasks are needed, tap "**Details**" to go back. While you can't flag all of the subtasks from the main Details page, you can toggle on "**Flagged**" to flag the parent. Doing so won't flag all the subtasks underneath, only the parent. Toggle it back off to unflag it. Hit "**Done**" to finalize things.

Tag a Contact in the Reminder App

- Tap on your selected or new reminder to bring up the information button, then tap that (*i*) to bring up the Details settings, where you can add notes and configure a handful of parameters.
- Select the toggle for "**Remind me when messaging,**" so it's on, tap the new "**Choose Person**" option, then pick a contact from the list that pops up, either by browsing or searching.
- After doing so, you'll return to the reminder's settings with your contact tagged under the toggle.
- If you want to choose another person, tap "**Edit**," then tap another contact from the list. When satisfied with your selection, tap "**Done**." You'll see your chosen contact tagged on the reminder in any list view of the app itself, a helpful way to quickly identify which reminders have messaging tags.

CHAPTER EIGHT

Enable/Disable Swipe Typing

- Launch the **Settings**
- Select **General**.
- Scroll down and tap **Keyboard**.
- Next, scroll down to Slide to Type and disable it. If you need to enable it, you can basically enable it once more.
- If you need the delete key to remove one letter rather than the entire word, go to **Delete Slide-to-Type by Word** and disable it.

How to Use Swipe Type

Swipe-typing is enabled by default. All you have to do to get swiping is simply start swiping.

- Spot a finger on your screen and drag it over the letters of the word you need to type. Let's say you want to type "mind," you would tap on the "m" key, and drag your finger over the "i," "n," and "d" letters in successive order. The keyboard will, at that point, foresee the word you're typing.

- The advantage of swipe-typing is that it's generally a lot quicker than tapping on each key in progression. After swiping, the keyboard will present three options for your swiped word, so you can tap to choose the one you need. However, if the middle prediction is right, start swiping your next word to auto-select it.
- Those predictions will get progressively accurate the more you utilize your keyboard. However, you can swap between tapping and swiping whenever, and there's no need to adjust any settings to change.

Set a Custom Name and Profile Picture via iMessage

- Open iMessage/Message App from the Home Screen.
- Tap on **Ellipsis (...)** located in the upper right corner of the screen.
- Tap on the **Edit Name** and **Photo** tab.
- Next, tap on **Edit** from the Profile photo
- You can choose between Apple Suggestions for Profile photo or the Animoji available.

- If you want to use the Suggestions option, you can set Profile photo by snapping a photo right direct from the camera app, or you may choose from your photo gallery.

To set Profile Picture using a captured image:

- Tap on the Camera icon from the Suggestion option.
- Capture an image.
- Once the image of choice is captured, move, and scale the captured image from the camera, make sure correctly crop the image to fit in the circular frame of the Profile Photo.
- Tap on **Use Photo**
- Select your filter of choice to change the appearance of the captured image.
- Tap "**Done**" to apply changes.

If you want to use the photos from your photo gallery on your device:

- Tap on the **All Photo** option and select the desired photo from photo albums
- Once the desired photo is selected, move and scale the photo to adjust its size making sure it fits in the circular frame, then
- Tap on **Choose**.
- Make necessary changes in appearance if desired by selecting the available filters.
- Tap "**Done**" to apply changes.

If you want to choose Animoji or personal Memoji:

- Select the Animoji or Memoji of your choice from the Animoji and Memoji from the choices available .You can also select a pose for the Animoji.
- Tap on **Next**.
- Move and Scale the selected Animoji or Memoji.
- Tap on **Choose**
- Select a Color for your Animoji Background
- Tap "**Done**" to apply changes.
- After every change made with the Profile Picture, you will notice a prompt "if you want to use this image in all places? Your ID and My Card in Contacts will be updated with this image" You can tap on either of the options "**Not now**" & "**Use**."
- Tap "**Done**" again. You will now see your desired Profile Photo.

Share Custom Name and Profile Photo

Having a Profile Picture and Profile Name on your iMessage Profile in iOS 13 does not necessarily mean that it will now be available for others to view or to be displayed. For privacy and security purpose, you still have the option of whether or not share your iMessage Profile. For additional information, there are two methods on how to share the iMessage profile:

Method 1:

- Open the iMessage/Message app
- Tap on Ellipsis (**…**) located in the upper right corner of the screen
- Tap on **Edit Name** and Photo option
- Toggle on the **Name and Photo Sharing** option
- Choose to **Share Automatically to Contacts Only** (Profile Name and Profile Picture will be shared automatically) or **Always ask** option (a prompt will appear if you want to share your iMessage Profile to a particular person).
- Tap "**Done**" to apply new changes.

Method 2:

- Go to **Settings** from the Home Screen
- Scroll down from the list of apps, and tap on **Messages**.
- Look for the **Share Name and Photo** option, then tap on it.
- Choose to **Share Automatically for Contacts Only** (Profile Name and Profile Picture will be shared automatically to your contacts) or **Always ask** option (a prompt appears

every time to ask if you want to share your iMessage Profile to a particular person).
- Tap "**Done**" to apply new changes.

Delete your iMessage Profile Image

- Go to the **Settings** app.
- Select **Messages** from the rundown.
- Choose the option tagged **Share Name & Photo**.
- Touch **Edit** below your current iMessage profile picture.
- On the following screen, touch **Edit**.
- Next, tap **Delete**, then select **Delete** from the popup menu to confirm the action.
- Tap "**Done**" to save the changes made.
- Your iMessage profile image will now appear blank.

Pair a DualShock 4 Controller with Your iPhone

- Go to your iPhone Settings and ensure that Bluetooth is on
- Grab your PS4 DualShock 4 controller
- Push and hold the PS button and share button at the same time for 5 seconds
- After 5 seconds you should see the lightbar start to blink
- Go back to your iPhone, and under Bluetooth, you should see "**DualShock 4 Wireless Controller**" listed
- Tap on it to connect
- Your PS4 DualShock 4 controller's light bar will turn pink once it has been successfully connected

Pair Xbox One Controller With iPhone

- Go to your iPhone Settings and ensure that Bluetooth is on
- Grab your Xbox One controller
- Press and hold the wireless button on your Xbox One controller for a few

seconds (the button is located at the top of the controller towards the back)
- The light on the Xbox button will begin to blink
- Go back to your iPhone, and under Bluetooth, you should see "**Xbox Wireless Controller.**"
- Tap on it to connect.
- If it has been successfully connected, the Xbox button's light will stop flashing and will remain lit.

Unpair DualShock 4/Xbox One S controller

- Launch **Settings** on your iPhone.
- Tap on **Bluetooth**.
- Locate your DualShock 4 or Xbox controller in the device list, and then touch the "*i*" button.
- Choose to **Forget this device**.
- Confirm the unpairing by tapping on **OK**.

How to Customize VoiceOver

VoiceOver is a function that reads out the screen so that even people with visual impairments can use the iPhone. The selected screen display will be read by the iPhone on behalf of the user.

You can also change the speed and pitch at which the screen display is read out using VoiceOver. Detailed settings can be changed in "**Settings app > Accessibility > VoiceOver**.

CHAPTER NINE

Scan Documents from the Files App

- Launch the Files app on your iPhone
- Touch the **Browse** tab at the bottom of the Files app.
- Touch the **More** button (three-dot icon) at the top of the display.

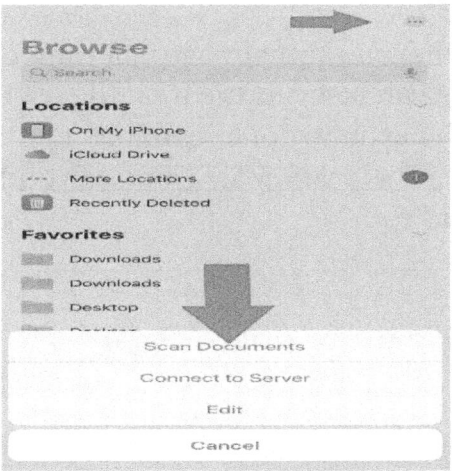

- Touch **Scan Documents**.
- Place your document in the viewer and touch the Capture button.
- You can decide to drag the corners to modify it, touch to **Retake** or touch to **Keep Scan**.

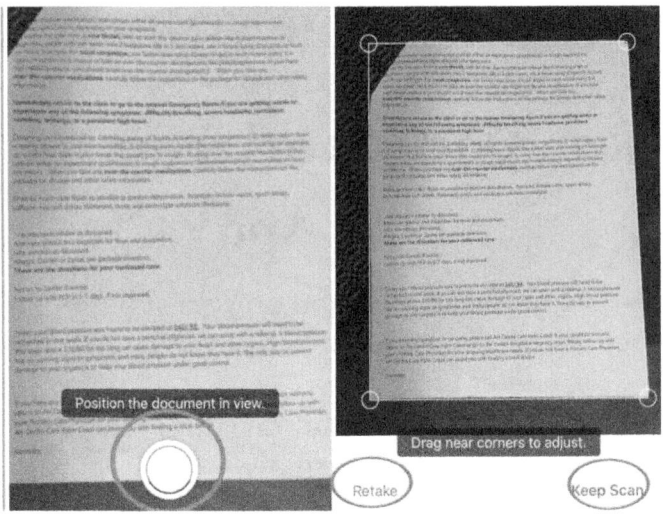

- If there's another page you want to scan, you can just capture it on the next screen.
- When you're done scanning, tap "**Save**."
- Select a location for your scan and touch "**Save**."

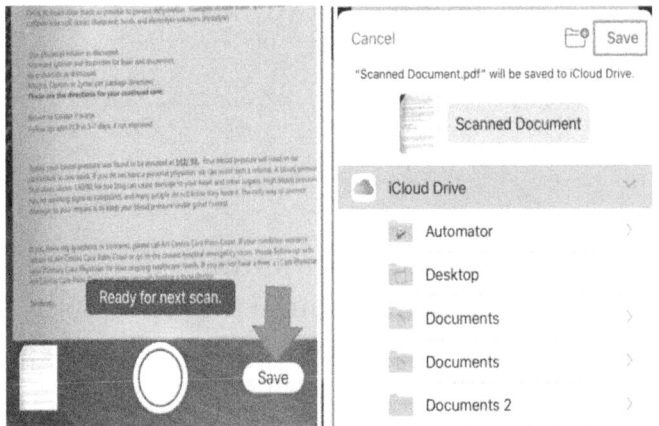

- You can also scan a document within a location like iCloud Drive or On My iPhone in the Files app.

- Tap the **More** button (three-dot icon) at the upper left and then follow the same steps above.

Save and Share Webpage as a PDF

- Launch the Safari app on your iPhone and visit any web page of your choice and let the page get loaded completely, else, it will not be able to save full page as PDF later on.
- Now press and hold the Home button and Side button at once to capture a screenshot on your iPhone in Safari.
- You can now see the preview of the screenshot taken on the bottom left corner, tap on the screenshot and then tap on **Full Page** option that's available on the right top corner.

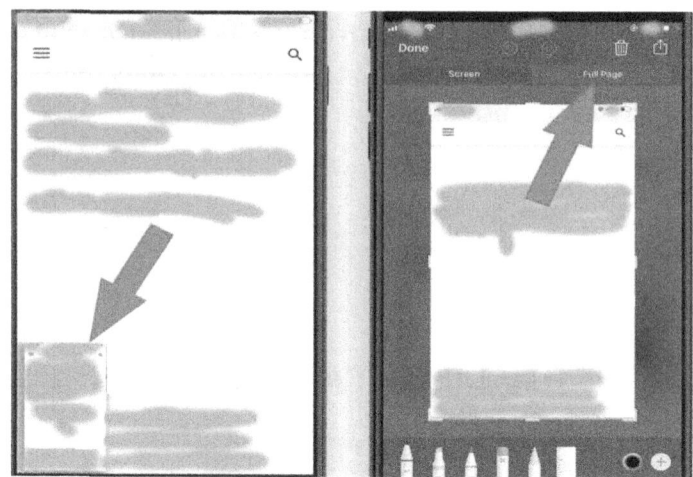

- Next, tap on "**Done**" and then select **Save PDF to Files**" option.

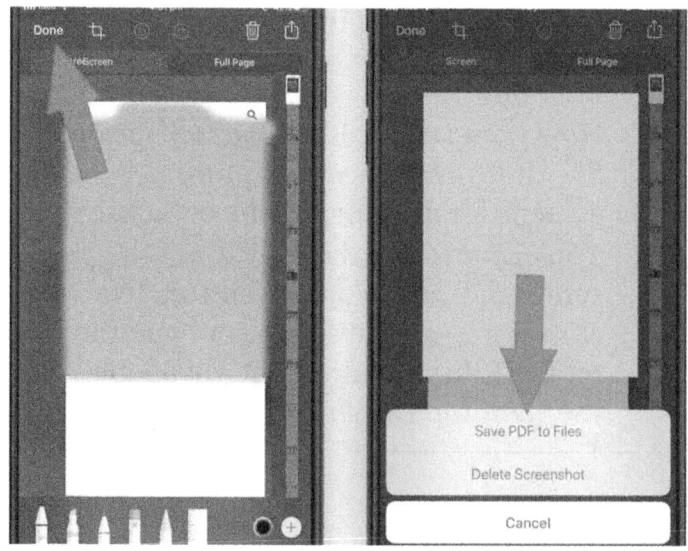

- Select any of the folders from "**On My iPhone**" or "**iCloud Drive**". If the desired folder isn't available, create one and then tap on "**Save**." This will save your PDF.

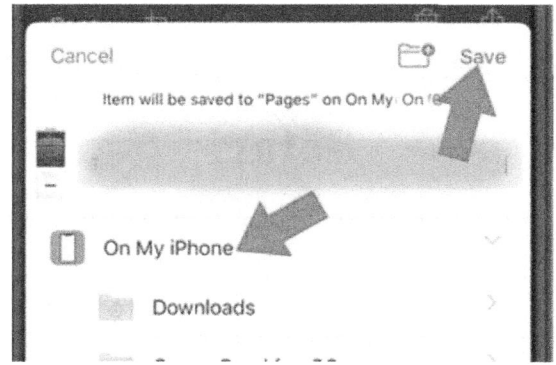

- If you want to share the PDF via Email or iMessage, after the third step, tap on the share button option available on the top right corner.

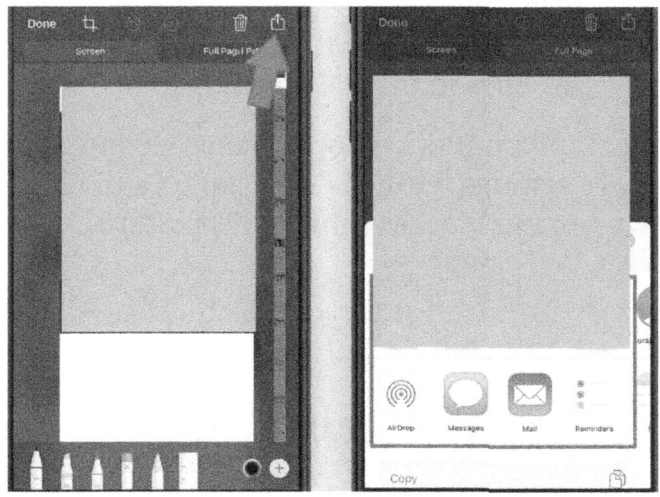

- Once done, select iMessage/Mail or any other platform, enter the recipient, and tap on "**Send**." That's it!

Enable Content Blockers in Safari

Content blockers offer a one-trick solution for prohibiting ads like popups and banners from stacking on websites you visit. They can likewise shield you from online tracking by deactivating cookies and scripts that sites try to load.

- Open the **Settings** app.
- Scroll down and tap **Safari**.
- Under **General**, touch **Content Blockers**.
- To activate content blockers, flip the switches to the ON position.

Note: Content Blockers option doesn't appear in Safari's settings until you've installed a third-party content blocker from the App Store.

Temporarily Disable Content Blockers in Safari

- Open Safari on your iPhone and go to the site in question.

- Tap the "**aA**" icon in the upper left corner of the screen to uncover the **Website View** menu.
- Tap **Turn Off Content Blockers**.
- If you only need to disable content blockers for a particular website, tap **Website Settings** in the **Website View** menu, and afterward flip the switch next to **Use Content Blockers** to the OFF position.

Access the Download Manager in Safari

- When you try to download a file on Safari, a little download icon is displayed in the upper right corner of the screen.
- You can tap the icon to check the status of your downloads, and tapping the magnifying glass next to the file will open its folder location.
- By default, files downloaded in Safari are stored in the "**Downloads**" section of the Files app. However, you can customize the storage location: go to the **Settings** app, select the **Safari** section, and tap **Downloads**. From this screen, you can select to store downloaded files in **iCloud Drive**, on your **iPhone**, or in another

location based on your personal preference.
- The Downloads screen in Safari settings has an option to "Remove download list items automatically after one day" (the default), "Upon successful download," or "Manually."

Change the Default Safari Download Location

- Open the **Settings** app
- Tap **Safari**
- Select **Downloads**. You would then be able to choose one of the recommended places or tap **"Other"** to pick another registry. Third-party apps might have the option to support this, so if your favored location is turned gray out, you may need to hang tight for a future app update.

How to Automatically Close All Open Safari Tabs

- Launch the **Settings** app.

- Scroll down and tap **Safari**.
- Locate the section tagged "**Tabs**" and select "**Close Tabs**."
- The default will be manual. Select the timeframe you want your tabs to close automatically.

Manually: Safari won't automatically close tabs.

After One Day: All open tabs will be cleared after 24 hours.

After One Week: All open tabs will be cleared in seven days' time.

After One Month: All open tabs will be cleared following a month.

Enable/Disable Limit Ad Tracking

- Launch the **Settings** app
- Tap **Privacy**.
- Find the **Advertising** option situated at the bottom of the page, and then search for the **Limit Ad Tracking** option.
- Flip the **Limit Ad Tracking** option to on or off base on preference.
- It ought to be noticed that you can generally re-enable ad tracking by following the means above, yet flipping

the relevant options on by tapping them to turn them green (on account of location-based tracking) and dark (for Limit Ad Tracking).

Turn On Voice Control

- Go to **Settings**.
- Touch **Accessibility**.
- Touch **Voice Control**.
- Switch Voice Control on. Since Voice Control is active, you'll see a blue microphone icon appear alongside the clock in the top left. This means Voice Control is on and continually tuning in for commands.
- Now, you can begin utilizing Voice Control; you presumably don't realize what commands are accessible to you. For an outline of what you can say and do, tap **Customize Commands**. There are many, numerous commands, and they're each split up into classifications. Tapping one will show all of you the acknowledged phrases that will trigger a particular action.
- You can likewise include commands, utilizing the **Create New Commands** option inside the **Customize Commands** page. To create a command Voice Control will notice, you'll need to

indicate the type of the action and the application where it is to be used before you work out the command itself.
- If you only need Voice Control to listen when you're staring at your phone, switch on the Attention Aware setting on the main Voice Control screen. At the point when your phone notices you're not staring any longer it, Voice Control will be switched to sleep; however, to use Voice Control without staring at your device, you'll need to say "Wake Up" before proceeding to your command.
- All things considered, there are two commands specifically you should be open to using: "Show Grid" and "Show Numbers." These commands will enable you to connect with anything on your iPhone's screen, regardless of whether there's no default phrase for what you're attempting to perform with Voice Control.

How to Block Email Senders

- To do this, first, make sure that the email address you want to block is linked to a contact in your phone
- Then block that contact by tapping on their name and selecting **Block this Caller**.
- Next, open the Settings app and tap **Mail**.

- Under the Threading header, tap **Blocked Sender Options**, then tap **Move to Trash**.

How to Unblock a Number on iPhone

- Go to **Settings** > **Phone** or launch **Settings** > **FaceTime**.
- Touch Call Blocking & Identification.
- While on the **Blocked Contacts** list, swipe right to left through the number, then touch **Unblock**.

Unblock People Who Text You

- If you had blocked someone in Messages, you could unblock the number in the Messages app to enable them to text you again.
- Go to **Settings**
- Tap **Messages**.
- Scroll down and tap **Blocked**.
- Swipe from right to left on the number you wish to unblock and then tap **Unblock**.

How to Add Contacts on iPhone

- Launch the Phone app.
- Touch **Contacts**.
- Touch the "+" icon situated at the top right-hand corner of the display.
- Input the details into the fields for the First Name and Last Name, respectively.
- Tap on **Add Phone**, and afterward enter the contact phone number.
- Tap on **Add Email**, and afterward type in the contact email address.
- Touch "**Done**" to save.
- Navigate or search the name on the Contacts to check if it was effectively saved. If you wish to add more contacts, simply follow the same process.

Set Up Voicemail on your iPhone

- Launch the Phone app. At the bottom of the phone window, you will see the Voicemail icon in the right corner. Select it to open up your visual voicemail.

- The voicemail screen should show a blank space with a button to Set up now in the middle of the screen. Select this. If you have used iPhone's voicemail service previously, you can sign in with your old password here to automatically access your old voicemails. If you have never made use of visual voicemail, you should create a password and re-enter it. Whenever completed, select "**Done**."
- Now your iPhone will show the Greeting screen. If you don't fancy the greeting, you can choose Default and afterward "**Done**" to skip this part. If you need to personalize your greeting, select **Custom**, and then **Record** to record your greeting and **Play** to repeat it. When you're happy with it, select "**Done**."
- Your iPhone voicemail is currently officially set up.

How to Merge Duplicate iPhone Contacts

- To merge duplicate contacts, simply open a contact and tap on the "**Edit**" button.
- Next, select the "**Link contacts**" option. This will open your contacts list. Simply

select the contacts you wish to merge with the current one. That's all!

Copy Contacts from Social Networks & Email

- Launch the Settings app.
- Tap **Passwords & Accounts**.
- Choose a social network or an email account
- Touch the pointer next to "**Contacts**" to turn on the function.
- Slide your finger upwards, beginning from the bottom of the screen to go to the home screen.

Set Up Emergency Medical ID

- Open the **Health** app
- Touch "**Medical ID**" at the bottom-right corner
- Next, tap on "**Create Medical ID**" to start adding your health info.

- On the following screen, enter all your medical information, including allergies, well-being conditions, emergency contact details, and any helpful notes. This will be valuable if there's an occurrence of an emergency, and anyone around you can rapidly access this information.
- After you are done with adding the details, switch ON "**Show When Locked**." This feature is optional yet exceptionally recommended. The reason is that all the info you have entered will be noticeable to others regardless of whether your iPhone is encrypted.
- That is all; you would now be able to leave the Health app and lock your iPhone. You can confirm whether it is working or not by swiping up to the Passcode screen and afterward tapping on **Emergency** and then tap on **Medical ID**.

CONCLUSION

The iPhone SE is an amazing device. It is my concern to teach you how to use the smartphone in an easy and understandable way without bluffing, and I hope you're satisfied with my level of input. I made this for you and presumable you can now do all configurations with your iPhone SE (2020). I hope you find this guide useful and insightful, and it has helped you to find solutions to the most important features you ever wanted. Good luck and cheers.

ABOUT AUTHOR

Aaron Madison is a computer jerk, researcher, and a gadget perfectionist who loves to have all the latest gadgets. He loves to teach people how to use their devices and maximize its potential; He knows how to satisfy gadgets freaks and where to look to satisfy the teeming number of tech lovers. Aaron likes teaching the most complicated of things and making it simple for users. Aaron always gives you an "awe "feeling. You have no option but to love him when he writes as he includes all the necessary details and information.

Made in the USA
Monee, IL
15 December 2020